THE HOME EDIT LIFE

THE HOME EDIT

life

The Complete Guide to
ORGANIZING ABSOLUTELY EVERYTHING
AT WORK, AT HOME *and* ON THE GO

CLEA SHEARER & JOANNA TEPLIN

PHOTOGRAPHS BY CLEA SHEARER

MITCHELL BEAZLEY

To the incredible people who surround us:
Our families and friends for putting up with us, our employees for their exceptional work, our managers and agents who tirelessly advocate on our behalf, our business managers who always let us stay at nice hotels, our lawyer for making sure we break zero laws, and the Clarkson Potter team for making our dreams a reality.

perfume

bath

candles

feminine

travel

Contents

Introduction

This book is for both those who love to organize in their free time and those who *want* to get organized but feel they just can't make the time. It's for the moms who are sick of looking at sippy cups in their cabinets and wish there was more room for champagne glasses. It's for those of us who go to work, sit at our desks, and continue to wonder how we always end up with so many pens that rarely have ink. It's for the craft lovers, the beauty product enthusiasts, and the jet-set travelers.

Basically, this book is for everyone. We wanted to create a book that shows you how to live the life you love without feeling bad about the things you own. We wanted to show you that being organized isn't limited to pantries, closets, and other rooms in your house. It also extends to your hobbies, your travel, and even your phone. Organizing is a lifestyle and mindset that anyone can adopt. Consider this book our 360-degree approach to help you contain the chaos of your life and all the contents that come with it—whatever that may be.

Alright, now that we have that covered, it's time to step inside and leave any guilt you might have about owning things at the door . . . except can you maybe take your shoes off first? Thanks!

PART 1

Adopting the 360 Mindset

We closed our first book promising that our method would help you organize—and *maintain*—your space. But you can only lead a horse to water; you can't make it drink (is there any point in researching the origins of this quote? Wikipedia will surely suggest it's Drake). We were a bit unsure how many people would put our method to work. Suffice it to say, we were STUNNED by the response, and the amount of organized spaces that quickly ensued. We felt like proud Instagram moms seeing all our followers tackle their closets, mudrooms, hard-to-reach shelves, and pantries.

Although . . . didn't we explicitly warn against immediately organizing your pantry before getting your feet wet by tidying smaller spaces? Every time we saw someone tag us in an Instagram story where every single item in their pantry had been taken out and piled all over the kitchen, with the caption, "Just received my book in the mail! Getting started!" we wanted to scream, "NOOOOOO!!! DON'T DOOOOOO ITTTTTTTT!" We're very much hoping all those ambitious go-getters made it out unscathed and didn't end up crouched in a corner crying. Even *we* have ended up crying over a complicated pantry! Okay, not exactly *crying*, but certainly taking panicked shallow breaths and reciting, "Just keep swimming, just keep swimming, just keep swimming."

true story

It took us eight-plus hours to organize Constance Zimmer's pantry because we were having such a hard time with its dimensions. She actually said goodbye and left us at the house while she went to a holiday party. We were still there at midnight when she got home.

We promise we're not trying to take away your organizing fun, but we do want to reiterate that starting small and working your way up is the best way to ensure a successfully organized space. Starting on a drawer might seem like an insignificant project, but it can be just as transformative as organizing a larger space (and *what* is better than an organized bathroom drawer?!), helping to eliminate common hassles and improve your everyday life. In other words, no more rummaging around for a hair tie, or trying to find a pen to sign a permission slip. Have we sold you on starting small yet?

Rebranding the NO-JUNK DRAWER

So what if a drawer holds random items? As long as everything is contained and categorized, and makes sense in your daily routine, that's all that matters. Organization isn't one size fits all, and customizing spaces to your needs is the golden ticket.

TOP 5 SURPRISES
from Book One

1. **A lot of people took the book on vacation.** To a beach! To read about organizing! This is truly shocking, and we can only assume the bookstore was sold out of all thrilling romantic murder mysteries.

2. **People checked out copies of our book at their local libraries.** Not only were we delighted that folks patronize their libraries, but we were also so flattered that they put holds on *our* book and then *waited for weeks.* We received screenshots of library waiting lists from all over the world!

3. **Kids like organizing.** And not just the ones we gave birth to! We saw so many kids at our book tour events who came with homemade signs or photos of their organizing projects to show us. Naturally, we told all their parents (1) you're welcome, and (2) do their kids want a job?

4. **According to our tagged photos on Instagram, far more dogs like the book than cats.** This is not a scientific poll and we would require more data to accurately report findings, but we definitely need to shore up the cat community.

5. **OUR BOOK HIT THE *NEW YORK TIMES* BESTSELLER LIST!!!** This is something we will continue to be excited about for the rest of our lives and will likely add to our tombstones. We are *this close* to making our husbands introduce us as their *New York Times* bestselling wives. A huge thanks to our readers and fans for supporting the book from day one!

One thing that became abundantly clear, however, is that our first book appealed to both those who already liked to organize *and* those who needed a bit more help getting started. Some folks told us we were speaking their love language, and others felt it was a book filled with foreign concepts, but happily accepted the challenge anyway. Some people read the book with a highlighter in hand, and others just looked at the pictures. There's no right or wrong way—we're just happy so many people appreciate home organization. We kind of thought it was just us!

     Another thing we learned: There were a few pages that received by *far* the most attention. The first was our Low-Bar Lifestyle rules to live by. For those of you who need a refresher on our life's motto, this means we set the bar very *low* (as in, on the floor) so we can feel accomplished at all times. We give ourselves gold stars for remembering to feed our kids and getting dressed in the morning. It's amazing how many goals you can achieve when your expectations are that low.

TOP 5 LOW-BAR LIFESTYLE
Submissions

We asked you to send us your own Low-Bar Lifestyle moments, and WOW, DID YOU DELIVER:

1. "Wine is fruit. . . . You have eaten a full serving for every glass of wine. Not only are you full of antioxidants, but you are also actively combating scurvy."

2. "If the kids are screaming, it means they are breathing."

3. "Sometimes I feed my kids cereal for dinner and hype it like Oprah. 'YOU GET CEREAL! AND YOU GET CEREAL! EVERYONE GETS CEREAL!'"

4. "I don't spend much time inside the gym, but I spend a long time in the [gym] parking lot looking at Instagram, so I feel good about the total time spent."

5. "I add ice cubes to sparkling wine for extra hydration."*

*Clea's personal submission, sorry not sorry.

THE NO-GUILT LIFE

The common thread between the Low-Bar Lifestyle and our other motto, "It's okay to get rid of things," is the notion that when it comes to your stuff, you can kick your guilt to the curb. In creating the Low-Bar Lifestyle, we wanted to foster a community that championed even the smallest amount of effort. Like maybe you washed your hair. So what if you didn't blow-dry it (that would be a significantly higher bar)? It's *clean*, and that counts.

    In the same way that we don't want you to feel guilty about using dry shampoo for the fifth day in a row, we also don't want you to feel guilty when it comes to editing your items. After all, you should fill your home with only the things you like, need, or find sentimental. Here are a few examples.

THINGS YOU MIGHT LIKE	*THINGS YOU MIGHT NEED*	*THINGS YOU MIGHT FIND SENTIMENTAL*
Candles	Batteries	Childhood items
Clothing	Documents	Family heirlooms
Framed photos	Hand soap	Kids' artwork
Guitars	Lightbulbs	Notes and cards
Jewelry	Tax returns	Old photos
Vases	Toilet plunger	Wedding dress

An Incomplete List of

THINGS YOU THINK YOU NEED
but 99 Percent of the Time DO *NOT*

1. Pumpkin puree that will expire before next Thanksgiving (you didn't make that pie last year, either!)

2. Same goes for those cans of condensed milk

3. Souvenir cups from theme parks (that's what photos are for—your old soda cup is not a memory)

4. Anything that's missing a part (you are probably not going to a repair store to fix your blender—just get a new one you will use)

5. Every vase that has ever arrived with a floral delivery

When assessing whether to keep a particular item, put yourself to the test and consider which bucket it might fall into. If you can safely say that YES, you like it (maybe you haven't worn it recently, but this is your reminder to put that sweater into the rotation), or YES, you still need to hold on to it (hey, we all need toilet plungers), or YES, it's special to you (your child put some extra thought into that rock they painted for Mother's Day)—then by our measure, it can stay. Which brings us to our next point about the No-Guilt Life . . .

IT'S OKAY TO OWN THINGS.

ONCE MORE FOR THE
PEOPLE IN THE BACK!

IT'S.
OKAY.
TO.
OWN.
THINGS.

24

We are *so* proud of everyone's efforts to declutter their homes. It's a critical piece of the organizing process. Once you edit your items using the criteria on page 20, what's left are the items that matter to you (that plunger might even matter one day!). And so you should feel *absolutely no guilt* about owning the items that comprise your life.

Why fight the fact that your newborn needs a closet full of diapers, or your teenager needs a closet full of sports equipment? Resisting your reality instead of embracing it is unproductive and ultimately not useful. You're better off spending your time and energy looking for an organizing solution that accommodates all the components of your life rather than trying to live like someone else.

ORGANIZATION *vs.* MINIMALISM

Organization is often conflated with minimalism, when in fact, they are two very different things. You might define minimalism as living with less, while organization is an efficient and orderly arrangement of things or tasks. *Minimalism is a design style and a lifestyle choice.* But to be organized does not mean you must inherently own fewer things. It just means you need to be thoughtful about what you *do* own. You need to treat your *things* and your *space* with equal respect. An article once described us as "the organizing pros who let you keep more stuff." It made us laugh, but it also rang true. We want to help people live within their boundaries, rather than make them throw everything out. Because you can't own everything, but you can own plenty of things. Plus, if you mindlessly throw everything out, then you risk having to replace some of those things that you really did need, which is more wasteful than finding an appropriate solution for accommodating how you really live.

THE GOLDEN RULE: 80/20

One of our core beliefs is that you get the item or you get the space, but you don't get both. Everything you own takes up a certain amount of physical space, and eventually, even the largest home will run out of square footage. So how do you avoid that doomsday scenario? By making sure you live by our 80/20 philosophy: Keep your home no more than 80 percent full, and reserve at least 20 percent for breathing room. Using *all* the available space in your home is a bit like eating until you are overly full. It's as uncomfortable for your belt buckle as it is for your closets. And what if you want dessert? Or an extra pair of shoes? When you have no breathing room, you have no options, and that's just no way to live.

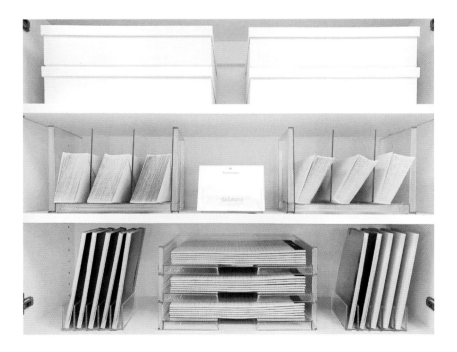

Top 5 Tips to AVOID
RUNNING OUT OF SPACE

1. Never buy more hangers! You get what you get and you don't get upset.

2. Contain everything so you know when you've exceeded your designated space.

3. With every new purchase, ask yourself, "Where is this going to live?" If you don't have an answer, it doesn't go home with you.

4. Set aside time once or twice a year to revisit and edit your spaces.

5. Wear a shock collar that physically stops you from leaving the house and buying more items.

As you begin to approach the 80 percent threshold, you'll notice things don't fit like they used to: You start cramming things into drawers, fighting with your pantry, and secretly wondering if you can store your winter coats in your daughter's closet. None of these things feels good, and it quickly becomes a puzzle too frustrating to solve. And that's what we're here for! We can help you solve your space while still embracing all the things you need, want, or use in your life. Whether you have it because you have kids, or you use it for work, or it simply makes you happy to look at—you get our official green light and approval to own said item. As long as you can store it appropriately without encroaching on the rest of your home, we see no reason to live with less if that doesn't work for you.

THE 360 APPROACH

When we say it's okay to own things, we mean *all* types of things. Organization is as much a mental activity as it is a physical one. And if you're going to be thorough, you need to *also* be prepared to face your issues, determine your priorities, and in some cases, own the upkeep. So before embarking on a project, it's helpful to ask yourself some questions and dig a little deeper. . . . (DISCLAIMER: We are NOT therapists, we just play one on Instagram.)

Let's start with the WHY. Why are you organizing this particular space? For instance, is it because your garage is a disaster and you can't find anything in it, or is it because you've always wanted cabinets devoted *just* to your Christmas decorations? Or perhaps you just sent your child off to college. Are you wanting to tackle their leftover clutter, or repurpose their room into the craft closet you've always wanted? (Go ahead, empty nesters, fly free!) There's no wrong answer here! And to be perfectly honest, a room filled with organized Christmas decorations or craft supplies sounds like heaven on Earth. The important thing is to understand your motivation from the outset and tackle each project with that motivation in mind. This way you can set up an achievable plan with realistic goals.

Now for the WHO. We like to ask ourselves, "Is this a ME issue, a WE issue, or a THEM issue?" Half the time, when we organize a space for a client, or even in our own homes, we need to admit we are going the extra mile because it satisfies *us*, not because it's a necessary part of the system. Lining up granola bars to be perfectly straight, making sure labels in the bathroom cabinet are all facing the same way, evenly spacing out closet hangers: These are ME issues—we do these things to satisfy ourselves. And you might feel inclined to take organizing to the extreme to satisfy yourself, too. In which case, you need to determine what you can reasonably expect from the members of your household, and whether you are

THE HOME EDIT LIFE

okay owning all granola-bar-straightening tasks. We don't expect our kids to line up their crayons by color, but we do expect them to place them in the container. There's nothing wrong with holding your family accountable for simple tasks like putting things back where they belong. And if they continually refuse, then you'll know that it's not a ME issue, it's a THEM issue.

Many of our clients have come to us with THEM issues that they need help tackling. And we're here to say that IT'S ABSOLUTELY DOABLE! For instance, maybe you've designated hooks for each member of the family in your mudroom and helpfully labeled them in your *very* nice handwriting, but no matter how many times you ask, they keep throwing their items on the bench. The system may be too complex for them. Instead of assuming that your kids are monsters and your husband is a mess, try tweaking the system so it works for them—and thus you.

Here's a solution for the previous example: Instead of hooks, try floor bins. They look nice, conceal items in an entryway, and give your family members a place to drop their things, which they are already really, really good at doing.

If something is a WE issue, it means the entire household needs to own the maintenance and upkeep. These systems need to be ingrained in everyone's minds so they become second nature. And when organization becomes second nature, a fairy gets its wings. For those who claim their family/roommate/partner will never get on board with an organized house, we present you with the silverware drawer. Every single person above the age of three agrees to respect an organized silverware drawer. It's very clear where to find a fork and where to put away the spoons, and as long as it's in the utensil holder, it doesn't have to be lined up perfectly (and if it does, it's probably a ME issue). We often cite this example because without realizing it, everyone in the household is already agreeing to this simple act of organization. And you know what we always say about starting with a drawer! If they can maintain a drawer, they can maintain much more. (By the way, unexpected rhymes about organizing *also* result in fairies getting their wings.)

KNOW THYSELF

We are not shy when it comes to sharing our own issues (although our mothers would prefer we exercise a bit more discretion before broadcasting all our weirdness to the world) because we own them through thick and thin: our strengths (organizing) as well as our weaknesses (everything else). And we've found that acknowledging our hang-ups helps our fans and followers navigate their own. Or maybe it just makes people feel better about themselves since we are such a hot mess . . . whatever the reason, we are happy to oblige. And since everyone seems to enjoy our particular brand of neurosis, we thought it might be helpful to put together a list you can reference any time you need a pick-me-up.

If you take the Enneagram Institute test, it reveals a LOT OF INFO. When we took it, we received so much clarity and insight into both the good and the . . . *less good* sides of our personalities. And it turns out it's pretty helpful to know thyself (this one is from Socrates, not Drake) before embarking on the process of organizing your life. Understanding your triggers, your underlying motivations, your lines in the sand might prevent you from hysterically crying over a sentimental pile of sippy cups.

Turns Out, We're an
ACQUIRED TASTE

CLEA
Type 3
(Achiever)

In brief: Self-assured, competent, ambitious, charming (OH STOP! Go on . . .), authentic, poised, overly concerned with their image and what people think (uh . . .), workaholic, competitive (okay really, stop)

Motivations: Want to be affirmed, distinguish themselves from others, have attention, be admired, and impress others (super-cool chill personality . . . JK, this is basically the least chill personality).

Famous 3s: The best part is that they tell you which celebrities are similar. The list for 3s starts off GREAT with Oprah, Reese Witherspoon, Paul McCartney, and Madonna, but *quickly* careens off course with Bernie Madoff and O. J. Simpson.

JOANNA
Type 4
(Individualist)

In brief: Self-aware, sensitive, reserved, emotionally honest, creative (so far, so good!), moody, self-conscious (well, there goes that), self-indulgent, dramatic, disdainful (why did we do this to ourselves?)

Motivations: To express themselves and their individuality, surround themselves with beauty to maintain their mood and feelings, withdraw to protect their self-image, take care of emotional needs before tending to anything else

Famous 4s: Fours have a less controversial celebrity list that includes Bob Dylan, Miles Davis, and Joni Mitchell, but does take an odd turn with magician Criss Angel.

TAKE A TEST

The way you know your Enneagram number is correct is if you modestly concur with the positives, and admit, " . . . Yeah, I guess that's me" when it comes to the negatives. And while it is not particularly fun to discover you share personality traits with O. J., it *is* helpful to gain some personal insight. The way you approach situations and interact with people comes into crystal-clear focus. In our experience, understanding that we are type 3 and type 4 helps us to be better friends, more communicative business partners, and more strategic when we are organizing for a client. Lucky for us, 3s and 4s are a complementary pair because each brings attributes that the other lacks to the table. And we didn't need the test to tell us this, but it's extra reassuring that they consider our coupling to be "notable for its energy, flair, sense of style, and enjoyment of the finer things in life" (you know we are aspiring fancy hotel bloggers). It goes on to say, "They'll feel a connection that goes beyond words or reason, like they have known each other from a previous existence, like a soul mate." We're not crying, we have allergies.

Take a personality test—any test—to help you gain clarity on what makes you tick. Try convincing other household members to take a test, too, so you can better understand them. Numbers not your thing? Maybe you prefer astrology . . . or try sorting yourself into a Hogwarts house—it's surprisingly accurate even if you are *not* a Harry Potter enthusiast (your loss). Clea would certainly be in Gryffindor with her determination, bravery, ambition, and social skills. Joanna is a Hufflepuff: hardworking, dedicated, patient, and loyal, with a strong moral code. Our point is, there's so much we can learn about our own behaviors, and the behaviors of those around us, which can inform our actions and decision-making.

And remember that it's okay for you to live with people who are vastly different from you—that's what makes the world go round. One thing you might have noticed if you have been following us for a while is that we are simultaneously complete opposites and the exact same person. It's what allows us to spend an infinite amount of time together without ever getting sick of each other. Seriously, we *choose* to share a hotel room after spending all day sitting side by side folding clothes in a client's closet. Our personalities, skills, and abilities complement and contrast each other with just the right balance. But our personality traits don't just make us good hotel roommates—they make us good teammates.

THINGS WE ALWAYS AGREE ON

1. Huge life-altering decisions that would normally require lengthy conversations, discussion, and compromise. Nope! We can usually wrap up monumental choices (such as starting a business) over lunch.

2. TV programming. This might seem like a small thing, but imagine sharing a living space with someone who *didn't* want to watch four straight hours of *Shark Tank*.

3. Getting to the airport three hours early is a necessity.

4. Being barefoot in public is unacceptable.

5. Better safe than sorry, *always*.

6. Escape rooms are the worst form of entertainment ever created.

7. Two kids maximum. The door is not just closed, it's sealed tight and drywalled.

8. Calories don't count on an airplane, in an airport, or after ten p.m.

9. Better to share a five-star hotel room than to have two rooms that aren't as nice.

10. Separation anxiety kicks in after being apart for twenty-four hours.

We're different from each other, and that's a good thing! We rely on each other's individual strengths to take the lead when needed, and to help balance our independent weaknesses. Being cognizant of these strengths and weaknesses allows us to work efficiently, and divide and conquer with each project. For instance, Clea likes creating big Instagrammable moments (ahem, see test results on page 36 about needing attention), while Joanna likes sitting on the floor carefully sorting the smallest bits and pieces (remember that part about being dedicated and patient?). Understanding our own motivations, what we each do best, and why we gravitate to certain aspects of a project is enormously helpful. It allows us to complete a project without ego, frustration, or even a question when Clea takes over organizing a shoe wall and Joanna spends five hours sorting jewelry into drawers. The same can be said about anyone you live with, whether a friend, a spouse or partner, or children. Recognizing your differences can be a stepping-stone for maintaining peace and organization in the home.

TYPICAL DIVISIONS *of* LABOR

IN A PLAYROOM

Clea: Color-coordinating books and merchandising the shelves
Joanna: Separating out doll pieces and craft supplies

IN A CLOSET

Clea: Displaying shoes and handbags
Joanna: Folding clothes

IN A BATHROOM

Clea: Organizing makeup into an acrylic tower
Joanna: Setting up a "daily" drawer

IN A PANTRY

Clea: Creating a canister collection for a focal point
Joanna: Setting up a tea station

Like clockwork, we fall into our distinct and separate roles every time. And once you start your organizing journey, you, *too,* will likely gravitate to the aspects that excite you most. You might be a Clea who likes the big picture, or you might be a Joanna who likes the granular pieces. You will still get the end result you want, but your approach will be very different. And accepting the type of organizer you are will help make the process fun rather than frustrating.

So while we're taking quizzes and sorting ourselves into numbers and signs and wizarding school houses (it's really so much cooler than it sounds), why don't we pause to take the quiz that matters *most*: Where are you on the organizing spectrum? To put it another way, are you a Clea or a Joanna? You might be saying, "I didn't ask to be either of you!" Well, you and us both—life is not easy!

ARE YOU A CLEA
OR A JOANNA?

1. **Your house is . . .**
   a. Full of colors and patterns—the more, the merrier.
   b. Black and white, with occasional rainbows if the situation warrants it.
   c. It doesn't matter, let someone else choose.

2. **Your favorite activity is . . .**
   a. Going to the spa.
   b. House-hunting.
   c. Escape rooms.

3. **You've moved . . .**
   a. Into your forever home.
   b. Again and again—you've never understood the phrase "forever home."
   c. For the last time—moving is too stressful.

4. **When your kids yell "Daddy!!" you . . .**
   a. Are delighted they didn't yell "Mommy."
   b. Are delighted they didn't yell "Mommy," so you pour yourself a glass of champagne.
   c. Kindly respond, "What do you need?"

5. **If you ever go to jail, it'll be because . . .**
   a. A kid on the playground climbed UP the slide, and slides are supposed to be for going DOWN.
   b. Someone slurped milk from their cereal bowl.
   c. You'd never do anything that would put you in jail.

6. **You've told all your friends and family that if you ever get kidnapped, you will text them with . . .**
   a. The poop emoji (you would NEVER use it under any other circumstances).
   b. "R u at the gym?" (the gym is a questionable red flag, and "R u" means "call 911").
   c. The thought has never crossed your mind.

7. **Your ideal vacation is . . .**
   a. Blackberry Farm with no TV, nowhere to be, and the most incredible food around the clock.
   b. London . . . they serve champagne with breakfast and there's endless shopping.
   c. Relaxing on a sunny beach with sand between your toes.

8. **You're most paranoid about . . .**
   a. Illegally leaving Canada with a granola bar without DECLARING THE FRUIT AND NUTS.
   b. Expiration dates and foodborne illnesses.
   c. World catastrophes (i.e., things that are not food-related).

9. **You have a free morning, so you . . .**
   a. Work out.
   b. Sleep.
   c. Volunteer at your child's school.

10. **If you won a million dollars, you would . . .**
    a. Buy $999,990 of blue and white throw pillows and put $10 toward savings.
    b. Immediately sell your home and use an extra $999,990 to purchase your next house . . . then put $10 in savings.
    c. Do something responsible, like investing it for the future.

11. **On an airplane, you . . .**
    a. Have your neck pillow on, your business books in one hand, your bag of candy in another, and at least three blankets on your lap.
    b. Have your iPad out, your iPhone charging and connected to Wi-Fi, and your hand in the air requesting a drink.
    c. Sit back, relax, and take a nap until you land.

If you answered mostly A, you're a Joanna! You like things that are overly sweet and colorful, and because you are SO TENSE on the playground, you need a massage as often as possible.

If you answered mostly B, you're a Clea! You like black, white, and rainbows, you need stimulation full-time, and moving homes is your favorite hobby. You also have misophonia and the sound of someone blowing their nose or chewing gum might put you in the slammer, so heads up.

If you answered mostly C, you're cool, calm, and collected . . . and probably someone who would hate being on a flight with us.

Now that we all understand each other a bit better, let's dive into the Home Edit lifestyle, shall we?

PART 2

Organizing for How You Really Live

Same Process,
NEW MINDSET

We want to help you dig a little deeper into the *contents* that make up your life and fill your home. Because regardless of how large or small your home is, we all contend with *things*—it's undeniable. Kid things, work-related things, things we need, use, or love. We all struggle with where to put them, what to do with them, and how to contain them. But let us reiterate what we said earlier: It's *okay* to own things as long as you respect your items and respect your space (remember our 80/20 rule!). As long as you aren't cramming things into corners and filling your drawers to overflowing, there is likely a solution available, and we intend to help you find it. In this section, we're going to show you some of the most common items we come across, and do our best to guide you through the organizing process.

SAVE YOUR SANITY

Imagine you are running late for school drop-off and instead of wasting precious time trying to find your keys, they are exactly where you left them—in a drawer, right next to a permission slip that you barely remember signing the night before . . . that is due today. THIS IS THE MAGIC OF SYSTEMS AT WORK, PEOPLE! When you create systems that flow with your daily routine and the items that encompass it, life becomes easier to manage and can lead to a happier and clearer mind. And what's better than that?

START WITH SMART,

Then Make It Pretty

Much like starting small with a drawer, when you approach organizing, it helps to be systematic. We firmly believe the best way to organize any and every space is to *first* make it as functional as possible, *then* make it as beautiful as possible. It's imperative that you operate in this order because if you're only trying to make a space look good, it won't function properly, and it'll end up deteriorating. If you start with what's smart, you can always boost the style after the systems are in place. And trust us, you're bound to make it pretty anyway because you'll love your space more than ever.

When considering smart systems, it's helpful to think in terms of zones, the boundaries that will contain your different kinds of stuff. They can be large zones you set up in a pantry (such as cooking staples, food, and storage items), or small zones that section off a beauty supply drawer in your bathroom (such as cotton balls, makeup, nail polish, and face wipes). These thematic boundaries are both healthy and helpful. They not only give the items a designated space, but they also hold you accountable for not *exceeding* that space. And if you follow our zone principles, we promise you will set yourself up for success.

snacks

sweets

utensils

1. Contain the *entire* category. We *really* don't enjoy separating like items. Putting some snacks in one area and some in another is panic attack territory. You risk losing the items, or buying the items again because you can't take stock of everything at a glance. We like to say that all friends belong together, and no one gets left behind! Yes, we frequently talk about inanimate objects as if they are friends.

2. Create a flow that makes logical sense. Your goal is to create an order for your zones that's intuitive to follow. To use the pantry analogy again, the food zone would have a day-to-night flow, from breakfast items to dinner items, and snacks can flow into sweets. The cooking zone would have oils and vinegars next to the condiments, and be adjacent to baking supplies (these are all building blocks of cooking). Or think about setting up a playroom: You could create zones for how your child might use the space—a quiet zone for coloring and reading, and a play zone for building blocks and dress-up. Contextualizing each zone helps to strengthen the system because there is genuine *thought* behind each and every decision. The use case for your things is clear, so the system is less likely to fail.

3. Consider who is using the space. We say this a lot, but it's worth repeating. Where and how you position your zones is key to successful maintenance. Do you need to keep items on low shelves for your kids to reach by themselves, or on a high shelf out of their reach? Is the station by the front door easily accessible for every member of the household?

Considering these things in advance *might* (no promises) mean your children, spouse, partner, roommate, and more will actually adhere to your carefully thought-out organizing principles.

IT'S OKAY TO
OWN THINGS WHEN . . .

IT'S FOR YOUR SELF-CARE

HOW WE WELLNESS

MORNING BEVERAGE

Joanna: Decaf, or half-caf if it was a *wild* night

Clea: Two shots of espresso and keep them coming

DAILY WORKOUT

Joanna: Barre class or a run

Clea: There's nothing "daily" about a workout

NUTRITION

Joanna: Pretend vegan—only eats bread, bagels, tomatoes, cucumbers, pickles, capers, avocado, and french fries

Clea: The opposite—cheese, meat, fish, and vegetables

WELLNESS

Joanna: Doesn't believe in vitamins

Clea: Loads up on vitamins and never remembers to take them

MOMENT OF ZEN

Joanna: Bowl of Swedish Fish (not vegan . . .)

Clea: Bowl of champagne (holds more than a glass)

As you can see, self-care means different things for different people, but we support any and all of it. Getting to organize routines and rituals for our clients is a real treat, because it means we get to enhance their enjoyment. Sometimes they don't even *realize* their routine is an important and treasured part of their day until we suggest we honor it as such. And can you think of anything better than a SELF-CARE STATION? Most definitely not.

While you're home editing, use this time to think about enhancing your space to accommodate your own self-care routines. How can you create a section of your home devoted to your mental and physical self so you can better tackle the day? Whether that's a coffee station with everything ready to go or a yoga studio on a shelf, this might be the most rewarding organizing project of your life!

WHEN YOU'RE A MORNING PERSON

If you spend about five seconds on our Instagram page, it's clear how much we love a morning beverage station. Tea, coffee, cocoa . . . whatever the preference, these items are *very* fun to organize.

IN A DRAWER

Step 1: The multitude of teas was sorted by caffeine level, type of tea, and shape of the tea bag. Some were just oversize or oddly shaped, and they needed different compartments.

Step 2: The tea tins were lined up on their own because they already came with a perfect container that's both airtight and pretty to look at.

Step 3: Tea tools were organized next to sweeteners to complete the setup.

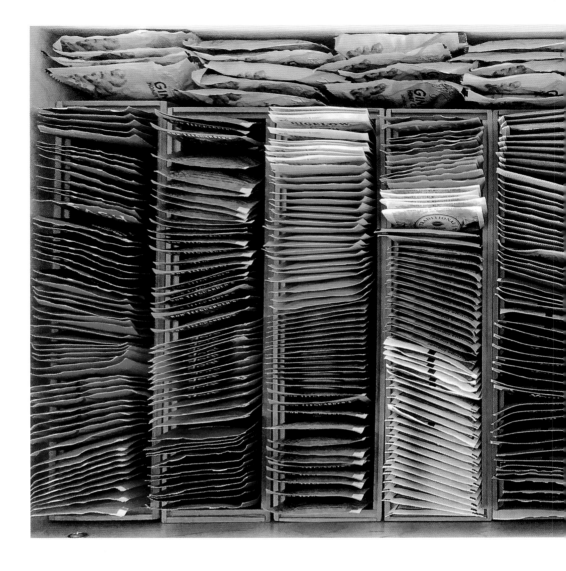

We are also very happy to line up tea bags in rainbow order, if the collection allows. The categories typically still make sense in color order since red packaging is often used for caffeinated tea, orange and yellow packaging for citrus-flavored tea, green packaging for green tea, and blue and purple packaging for nighttime herbal teas.

IT'S OKAY TO OWN THINGS WHEN . . .

Every now and then, we run in to tea bags without any exterior packaging (we're looking at you, Celestial Seasonings). In that case, we opt for round tea tins to store alongside the tea bags.

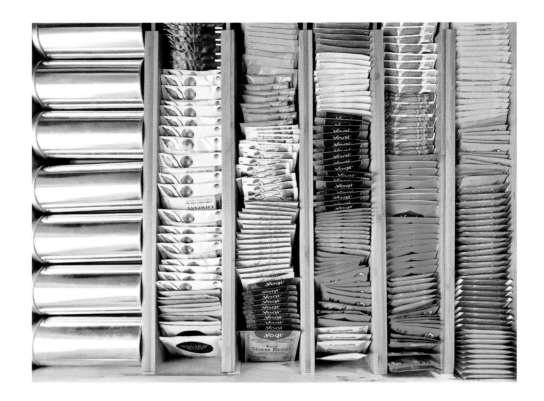

ON A SHELF

Step 1: After assessing the tea and coffee combinations, it was clear that canisters on the shelf were the perfect solution. We decided to go all out and turn this nook into a dedicated morning station.

Step 2: We added mugs, kettles, and smoothie supplies to accommodate *all* beverages.

IT'S OKAY TO OWN THINGS WHEN . . .

A FARM-FRESH FRIDGE

For many people, taking care of themselves revolves around a healthy diet. And we've seen firsthand that this means stocking the fridge with as many veggies, raw foods, and fresh herbs as possible. So when we see these contents, we organize with a mission: Support the healthy lifestyle (and take a lot of notes while doing it).

Step 1: Every fridge is begging for zones. . . . We divided this one into juice, dairy, prepped foods, spreads and sauces, meat and cheese, and fresh produce.

Step 2: Fresh herbs were also *begging* for some attention, and of course we were happy to oblige! We placed them in mason jars with a bit of water to keep them fresh, and organized them in the fridge door.

Step 3: We transferred out as much packaging as possible and opted for reusable containers. Eggs went into stackable organizers, milk and juice went into glass pitchers, and cut fruit went into glass food storage containers.

IT'S OKAY TO OWN THINGS WHEN . . .

We took a similar approach while organizing **Tiffani Thiessen**'s fridge. Many of the zones are the same, but we needed to account for larger quantities since Tiffani cooks so frequently. She also has gardens and chicken coops, and makes everything from scratch. We opted for a turntable (AKA lazy Susan) to hold the variety of herbs and flanked it with bins of homemade spreads, sauces, and preserved items. Ready-to-eat fruit is a fan favorite at snack time, and since the fruit doesn't last long, it was stored in open bowls.

      We often decant commonly used beverages, but for those with a penchant for pressed juices, a bin makes much more sense. The juice stays fresh until it's ready to be opened.

EXERCISE AT HOME

One of the defining factors in the age-old question, "Work out? Or skip it?" is ease. Whether it's finding a nearby gym, a yoga class you like, or having an easily accessible running route, you are much more likely to actually exercise if you can remove the "work" from a workout. Setting up a home gym is a great way to ensure you actually fit in a few active minutes in the middle of a busy day. It doesn't mean you need to invest in a treadmill or a StairMaster, but a few free weights and a yoga mat can go a long way toward your fitness goals. And we're very much looking forward to taking our own advice one day!

Step 1: We sorted the workout equipment into his and hers, so everyone has their own sets in labeled bins.

Step 2: A garage shelving unit was repurposed to hold everything in one place and get the items off the floor (with the exception of the giant free weights that we couldn't even lift).

Step 3: No station is complete without thinking through the before, middle, and after. Towels and water bottles were added to keep all workout necessities within arm's reach, and an exercise mat was placed on the floor to save a step.

If you don't have the space for a gym setup, or prefer a Pilates class to at-home resistance bands, you can still dedicate a spot for your supplies.

BATH AND BEAUTY BACK-STOCK

Busy people need a lot of back-stock, and honestly, not many people are busier than **Katy Perry**. Between touring, judging *American Idol*, and designing a footwear collection (just to name a few pastimes), there's little time to waste when it comes to needing daily essentials. Of *course* she needs extra Epsom salts and packs of probiotics—wellness can't wait, folks!

Step 1: We divided the shelving into zones for vitamins and wellness, bathroom back-stock and travel-size supplies, hair supplies, outdoor sprays, and bath salts.

Step 2: To make the most of the lower shelf (always the most important real estate), we used a combination of items from our branded line at The Container Store: the drawer unit stacked with our multipurpose bin on top, then *subdivided* both with our baby bins. Our goal was to keep the most-used items (like daily multivitamins) within reach so the systems felt functional and not frustrating. As a bonus, with the majority of items accounted for, we were able to give the items on higher shelves some breathing room.

Step 3: Once we had everything organized into their respective places, we moved the matching multiples to the front of each bin to add to the aesthetic. *Not* lining up all the tiny Listerines would have been an enormous missed opportunity.

For **Khloé Kardashian**'s back-stock, we decided to use stacking drawers, since they took the best advantage of the extra-deep shelves. These cabinets go from floor to ceiling, so we wanted the heaviest items toward the bottom (even if you're using a ladder, you never want heavy items to be above your head). Khloé is already extremely organized, so we just added our own touch to her already well-thought-out systems.

When we organized **Olivia Culpo**'s bathroom, our goal was similar to the previous examples: Keep as many items as possible within reach. She actually uses all of these! Daily! We kept holding up serums, cleansers, and eye creams, *positive* that at least a few of them would go on the discard pile. No such luck. We *did,* however, compromise on a bin for her mom (added to the top shelf) so she could gift her any additional incoming items.

As you can see from **Savannah Chrisley**'s bathroom closet, she *loves* products. But you can also see that (1) she has plenty of space to grow the categories, and (2) if she finds a face mask and a bubble bath soothing, we say she should keep it.

true story

While we were organizing Savannah's bathroom, she texted us pictures from Sephora to show that there would be plenty more makeup on the way!

SERIOUSLY
INTO
SUPPLEMENTS

In this day and age, if you tell us something might be even remotely beneficial, we are all ears. Turmeric tablets, you say? Sure. Collagen peptides in coffee? Sign us up. We're not sure what half of it actually *does*, but we are willing guinea pigs. And when our clients seem to have a stocked supply of supplements, oils, powders, and teas, we create a station to house everything in one place. Plus, lining up all the little bottles on turntables is very fun—five stars, highly recommend.

Step 1: The first step for every wellness cabinet is to determine what wellness means to you. Are the contents part of your daily routine, or an infrequent attempt at making matcha? If it's the latter . . . no judgment—we are personally guilty of it, too. But it also means you don't need to give up valuable real estate to something that's only occasionally used.

Step 2: Tea *was,* in fact, a staple for this household, so we set up a station on the bottom shelf with sweeteners, tea tins, and tea bags running down the center column.

Step 3: The middle shelf in this cabinet had the most height, so we opted to store all the small bottles of supplements on double turntables to take full advantage of the space.

If you're a smoothie lover and shake maker, we see you, too. You're the ones who are constantly asking us what to do with giant unruly tubs of protein powder that don't fit anywhere. We typically try to put these tubs with other bulky and oversize items. They never look good anyway, so at least they can all live together. Your heavy blenders, however, should stay down low (again, whenever possible, we try to keep heavy items on lower shelves).

We can't talk about wellness without talking about essential oils. We are relatively new to this world, and the first time we ever organized an essential oils collection, our client ran into the room saying, "You didn't touch the OREGANO oil, did you??" To which we replied, "WHAT?? WHICH ONE IS THAT!! WHAT IS GOING TO HAPPEN TO US?!" So let this be a cautionary tale that oregano oil burns. But look how happy they are, all lined up in rainbow order in a nail polish caddy! All's well that ends well(ness). (Couldn't resist.)

A close cousin of essential oils would be vitamins. If you don't have a cabinet to hold your large bottles of vitamin gummies, use a drawer! They easily lie down flat, and you can use drawer dividers to separate the categories.

HUM
BEAUTY STARTS FROM WITHIN

GUMMIES WITH BENEFITS

HAIR SWEET **HAIR**
for stronger, healthier hair*

biotin, folic acid, fo-ti,
b12, zinc and paba

DIETARY SUPPLEMENT
60 VEGAN BERRY GUMMY HEARTS

HUM
BEAUTY STARTS FROM WITHIN

GUMMIES WITH BENEFITS

GLOW SWEET **GLOW**
skin hydration for the ultimate glow*

hyaluronic acid,
vitamin C + E

DIETARY SUPPLEMENT
60 TANGERINE VEGAN GUMMIES

HUM
BEAUTY STARTS FROM WITHIN

GUMMIES WITH BENEFITS

GLOW SWEET **GLOW**
skin hydration for the ultimate glow*

hyaluronic acid,
vitamin C + E

DIETARY SUPPLEMENT
60 TANGERINE VEGAN GUMMIES

HUM
BEAUTY STARTS FROM WITHIN

RED CARPET™
for glowing skin & shiny hair*

black currant seed oil
gamma linolenic acid + vitamin E

DIETARY SUPPLEMENT
60 VEGETARIAN SOFTGELS

HUM
BEAUTY STARTS FROM WITHIN

RED CARPET®
for glowing skin & shiny hair*

black currant seed oil
gamma linolenic acid + vitamin E

DIETARY SUPPLEMENT
60 VEGETARIAN/VEGAN SOFTGELS

HUM
BEAUTY STARTS FROM WITHIN

ÜBER ENERGY®
supports consistent energy
through adrenal strength*

adaptogens, l-tyrosine, B5, B6

DIETARY SUPPLEMENT
60 VEGETARIAN CAPSULES

HUM
BEAUTY STARTS FROM WITHIN

**HERE COMES
THE SUN**
D3 without UV damage*

high potency vitamin D3

DIETARY SUPPLEMENT
60 SOFTGELS

HUM
BEAUTY STARTS FROM WITHIN

FLATTER ME
supports a flatter stomach
& healthy digestion*

18 full spectrum enzymes*

DIETARY SUPPLEMENT
60 VEGETARIAN/VEGAN CAPSULES

HUM
BEAUTY STARTS FROM WITHIN

GUT INSTINCT
friendly bacteria that benefit
your skin, health & beauty*

25 bn organisms, 10 strains

DIETARY SUPPLEMENT
30 VEGETARIAN/VEGAN CAPSULES

HUM
BEAUTY STARTS FROM WITHIN

**DAILY
CLEANSE®**
helps clear your skin
& body from toxins*

green algae & detox herbs

DIETARY SUPPLEMENT
60 VEGETARIAN/VEGAN CAPSULES

HUM
BEAUTY STARTS FROM WITHIN

BIG CHILL®
helps you cope with &
remove the signs of stress*

rhodiola rosea root extract

DIETARY SUPPLEMENT
60 VEGETARIAN/VEGAN CAPSULES

HUM
BEAUTY STARTS FROM WITHIN

**COLLAGEN
LOVE**
supports skin elasticity
and firmness*

collagen - types I, II & III

DIETARY SUPPLEMENT
90 CAPSULES

HUM
BEAUTY STARTS FROM WITHIN

WING MAN
widely used for liver detox
& dark circles*

silymarin from milk thistle

DIETARY SUPPLEMENT
60 VEGETARIAN/VEGAN CAPSULES

HUM
BEAUTY STARTS FROM WITHIN

MOODY BIRD®
your monthly ally vs. PMS*

dong quai & chaste berry (vitex)

DIETARY SUPPLEMENT
60 VEGETARIAN/VEGAN CAPSULES

HUM
BEAUTY STARTS FROM WITHIN

SKINNY BIRD®
our weight loss program

caralluma fimbriata, 5-HTP,
chromium, green tea leaf extract

DIETARY SUPPLEMENT
60 VEGETARIAN/VEGAN CAPSULES

IT'S OKAY TO
OWN THINGS WHEN . . .

YOU NEED TO STAY PLUGGED IN

Like it or not (and Joanna does *not* like it), we are living in the digital age. No one is taking away your pens and paper, but if it isn't typed and put in the cloud, does it even exist? If no one posted photos of an event on Instagram, did it even happen? If your phone is at 3% battery because you didn't pack a charger, will you survive? (That last one just sent a chill down Clea's spine.) The answer, of course, is NO, NO, and NO. So the mission, should you choose to accept it (Joanna does not), is to become an electronics survivalist. Let's start by determining your beginning or advanced status.

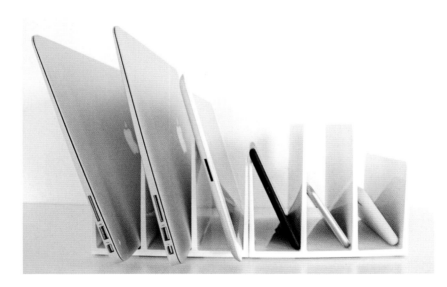

A DIGITAL AGE
OR DARK AGE QUIZ

1. **Your email address ends with . . .**
   a. @gmail.com.
   b. @sbcglobal.net.

2. **LOL means . . .**
   a. Laughing Out Loud.
   b. Lots of Love .

3. **When you travel you . . .**
   a. Have three phone chargers, backup battery packs, two types of headphones, an iPad, and a laptop.
   b. Have to borrow your child's tablet and watch *The Secret Life of Pets* because that's what has already been downloaded.

4. **In the car, you listen to . . .**
   a. Podcasts.
   b. "Alice the Camel," because it's the first song on your playlist and you haven't updated your music since your kids were two years old.

5. **When you send a text you . . .**
   a. Keep it short and sweet, with a 50 percent chance of an added emoji.
   b. Write what amounts to a lengthy email and sign it at the bottom.

If you answered mostly A, then CONGRATULATIONS on being part of the twenty-first century! This section of the book applies to you because you care about technology and all its various components. Fear not, we can help you wrap those cords and store your gadgets!

If you answered mostly B . . . well . . . don't feel bad. You just have a tiny bit of work to do to overcome your digital deficit. Take a highlighter to this next section, since you *definitely* aren't reading this book on an iPad!

true story

Clea's mom, Roberta, really did think LOL meant "Lots of Love," and once signed a condolence email with "LOL, Roberta."

EQUIPPED
WITH
ELECTRONICS

Of course **Khloé Kardashian** color coordinates everything, from her books to her electronics cabinets! She really is that perfect. And since we see eye to eye on all things organizing, working in her home is a dream come true. For these office cabinets, we wanted everything to be as accessible as possible to keep up (no pun intended, but let's just go with it) with her busy travel and work schedule.

Step 1: We emptied all the cabinets and started creating groupings of cameras, types of film, various headphones, and so on.

Step 2: Khloé cares about precision as much as we do, so we wanted to ensure that every inch of space was a perfect fit. These stackable bins allowed us to divide the categories while still keeping them grouped together.

Step 3: The camera collection was equally as prominent as the headphone and speaker collection, so we spread them out into their own cabinets to keep things from becoming cramped.

PHOTOGRAPHS LACHAPELLE LAND

HOTELS ARCHITECTURE & DESIGN

Christian Louboutin

Patricia Urquiola

WEAR YOUR FACE

PHILIP-LORCA diCORCIA

HUSTLERS

NOX

SNAPCHAT
SPECTACLES

MEMORY
CARDS

ACCESSORIES

ACCESS

CAMS
UIFILM

PIXPRO SL10
SMART LENS
LENSES

CAMERA
CHARGERS

TRIPOD
+ SELFIE STICK

CAMER

CAMERA
CHARGERS

SAMSUNG

GALAXY

FILM

FILM

FILM

FILM

IN NEED
OF A
CONSTANT
CHARGE

Are you one of the many people who panics when your phone gets below 50 percent battery life? And when the battery icon turns *RED,* do you start having heart palpitations? You're not alone. It's a common affliction, and there is a cure: charging stations. Create one in your home, in your office, in your car—wherever you spend the majority of your time. Keeping an extra charging cable handy is always a good idea (refer to the on-the-go chapter on page 92!), but if you already have stations set up in the places where you spend 75 percent of your time, you are 75 percent more likely to not have a nervous breakdown about being cut off from the world.

In this living room charging station, we took extra care to route and wrap the cords to obscure them from view. This way, tablets and phones are able to power up without creating an eyesore in the surrounding space.

If you have multiple devices, or want to create a charging station for the entire household to monitor screen time, using a letter divider (see page 77) and a large USB port does the trick! You're able to line up all the laptops, phones, and iPads and keep them stored overnight while charging.

If you have more than five devices in need of charging, line up as many letter dividers as you need to accommodate them.

EXTRA ELECTRONICS

Every device seems to come with extra cables, adapters, and accessories. Until the day comes when laptops, headphones, and mobile phones can all be charged by the same charging cable (WHY can't this madness be solved?? It seems like it shouldn't be that hard?!), having all options organized in one spot will at least simplify things. Plus, it will save your drawers from becoming a sea of twisted and tangled cords.

Step 1: All items were paired together with their friends: power adapters, cables, headphones, battery packs, and . . . we don't use this word lightly because it is SURELY the worst term ever invented . . . dongles.

Step 2: Have you recovered from the dongle reference? Barely? Same. Nevertheless, we persisted and stored said items in drawer compartments.

Step 3: For additional containment (and you *know* we love additional containment), we wrapped all the cables and headphones with cord ties to avoid tangling.

Cord organization doesn't have to be a dull affair. Plenty of options exist that add some extra flair. (This wasn't supposed to be a poem about organizing earbuds, but it turned into one, because that's how passionate we feel about the topic.)

PHOTO ARCHIVES

Unless you are a professional photographer, there's a good chance you haven't taken a photo on a device that isn't your phone in many, many years. And don't we all think we're Ansel Adamses in the making when we pull out our iPhone to take a picture of the sunset? For the most part, the photos we take, and the photos we share, are digital.

There are many reasons why storing and organizing your photos digitally is a good idea. (THINK ABOUT IT: Do you believe your children and/or future generations are going to appreciate the sentiment of the numerous heavy boxes, each filled to the brim with old photo albums that were kept in the basement for years? That you finally decided to hand off, right before moving to a retirement community in Boca Raton? They *probably* would have preferred it if you had digitized them back when the rest of the world did—but enjoy Boca, Mom.)

1. It's really, really, really easy to lose or damage paper of any kind. No one should ever have to carry around the guilt of losing Grandma Nancy's wedding photos due to the basement flooding. If it's digital, you can *always* print a hard copy. But if you lose the hard copy, you can never make it digital.

> **To anyone with the argument of things getting lost in "the cloud"—that's what hard drives are for.** For those that argue about privacy concerns . . . that is a fair point. But as people who share overly personal details at unflattering angles with all of Instagram on a daily basis, we obviously aren't concerned enough to change our ways.

$2.$ Photo albums and storage boxes take up a lot of valuable real estate. Most people rarely access these items, but still hold on to them for obvious sentimental reasons (and in our case, to remind future generations that at one point in time, we didn't look so tired). Similar to how carbs don't exist on vacation and calories don't count if someone *else* ordered the fries, digital photos leave no physical footprint, so you can load up without guilt.

$3.$ Let's be honest: Life is better sitting down. Wouldn't you prefer accessing *all* your photos with the click of a button, rather than having to pull heavy albums off a shelf or sifting through boxes? There's truly something magical about being able to type a keyword into a search bar and having the specific photo you are looking for pop up instantly (we'll get into this).

$4.$ YOU CAN EDIT TO YOUR HEART'S DESIRE. Whether you'd like to color-correct an old photo from 1975 or smooth out your wrinkles from 2019, there are a variety of photo-editing programs and apps that are easy to use and allow you to transform the quality of any photo without paying a professional service to do it for you.

Before we go over how to organize your digital photos, let's cover the basics.

PRE-DIGITAL AGE PHOTOS

These are the photos you are going to have to scan. Sorry, there's just no way around it. Will it be time-consuming? Probably. But will it be worth it? Most definitely.

Step 1: Invest in a good scanner. For the sake of efficiency, it needs to be a scanner with a tray that adjusts to size and allows photos to be fed through the device one after the other. Built-in color correction and editing is another plus. It's also important to choose one that will filter the photos to a designated folder on your desktop, which brings us to step 2. . . .

> **Start small.** And we really mean it this time. Don't think this will be a project that you can complete over the weekend. Because you can't. The best plan of action is to start with a single album or small photo box. Not just the first time, but every time you scan photos. This will make the process of uploading and categorizing your photos more manageable.

Step 2: Every scanner is different in its specific functionality, so we'll leave out the technical steps. However, the one thing that all decent scanners have in common is that they will route your photos to a single desktop folder. This folder (which is usually named after the scanner itself) is like purgatory for photos.

Step 3: Create a general "photo" folder on your desktop, and subfolders within it by category, preferably by year. Drag and drop photos from the scanner folder to the subfolders where they belong. You can always go back later and create subfolders within the subfolders, if necessary.

Step 4: Once the photos are in their correct folders, click the "info" button on each photo (if you are using iPhoto, look for the "i" button) and add keywords and tags that will make them easily searchable.

> **For tags and keywords,** it helps to think about how you will search for the photo in the future and go from there. For instance, if it's a photo from a family vacation to the beach, use the word "beach" as a tag. Even if you have multiple photos from various trips to the beach, they will at least be easier to filter through.

Step 5: Decide how you want to store the photos. Some people prefer to store photos on their desktop and import them onto a hard drive. Others prefer to keep their photos organized within iPhoto. Another option is using services like Dropbox and SmugMug that store your photos for you and require a password. Once you do your research, it comes down to preference and using a system that makes sense for you.

RAINBOW
IS RIGHT

If you read our first book, or have ever looked on our Instagram, or really know just the bare minimum about us . . . you know we have a penchant for rainbows. In our projects, in our lives, and—yes—on our phones. And nine times out of ten, when people get a glimpse of our home screen filled with apps in rainbow order, they first ask if we're crazy (the answer is yes), then they say there is no WAY we can find anything when the apps are organized by color. And MAN OH MAN, they probably did not anticipate the door they were opening with that statement, but such is life, and now they have to take a seat and listen to a full dissertation on why it's the *most* practical way to organize apps.

Before we tell you *how* to do it, we want to tell you *why* we do it. Oh, you thought you were immune from this lecture? Take a seat, friends. App icons are not arbitrarily picked, they are intentionally *designed*. Furthermore, they are designed to be recognized and remembered among a sea of other apps. This is the point in the (one-sided) conversation where we start quizzing people on their *own* apps and asking what color they are. So let's try a few . . . Facebook? Blue. Instagram? Purple. Spotify? Green. Uber? Black. Lyft? Pink. Waze? Blue. Try some of your own! You'll realize that you actually *do* know what they all look like. And for the multicolored app

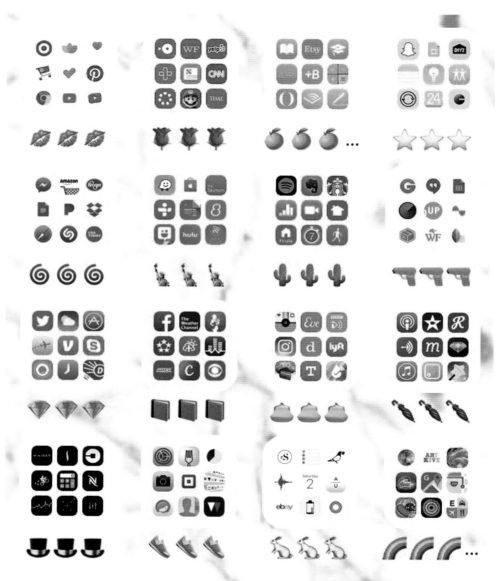

IT'S OKAY TO OWN THINGS WHEN . . .

icons without a clear color direction, they go in the rainbow section! The human brain is able to easily recognize things visually in the same way muscle memory develops: by repetition and use. If you use your apps, you will inherently know what they look like.

If you already have an organized phone, it's likely grouped by app type: Social, News, Travel, etc. And that's totally fine, if that works for you! But typically, it still requires a good bit of scrolling and scanning to find the app you need, since you don't have easy visual recognition. For those who do it alphabetically, bless you. You're crazier than we are, and we appreciate that.

Step 1: Every organizing project starts with an edit. We *all* have apps we don't use (us included) so get rid of any that are outdated or unused, since they only clutter your screen.

Step 2: Start grouping apps into folders organized by color. If you have more of a certain color (for example, blue and green app icons are very common), you can separate the apps with a white or black background from those that are a solid color.

Step 3: Place your most commonly used apps at the very top so you can spot them immediately. App arrangement within the color folder is a critical part of why this system works.

Step 4: Pick an emoji that color coordinates with the apps in the folder. This part is super fun, because when you find the perfect emoji, you get *very* excited and look around with satisfaction even though no one cares to recognize your achievement.

IT'S OKAY TO
OWN THINGS WHEN . . .

YOU'RE ALWAYS ON THE GO

This chapter hits a little too close to home. Although what do we know about being close to home? If we spend more than fourteen consecutive days in town, it's a miracle. The only thing that helps us get through our day-to-day work life and back-to-back trips is a series of finely tuned systems. Like our system for booking a flight:

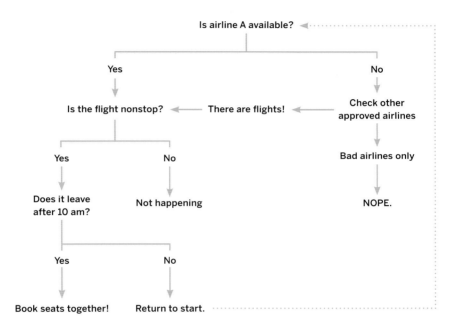

Shockingly, no one on our team will book our travel anymore. We ended up hiring a travel agent in order to maintain everyone's sanity (not to mention retain our employees).

We are also partial to making checklists for anything and everything. Maybe it's because we are two hundred years old, but it feels like if we don't write something down, it escapes our memory immediately. Even things that are habitual for us—like packing a suitcase—can feel like a monumental challenge without a proper list. Especially when you're exhausted and juggling a million other things. That's how you end up on a weeklong trip without a toothbrush or underwear.

[THE]
PACKING LIST

Not all items will apply to all people, and not all items will apply to all *trips,* but we always run through the same list when we travel for work and check off the applicable items. You might even annotate your packing lists to indicate what you wore and used and what you didn't wear and didn't use on the trip, so that your future packing lists will be more relevant to your needs.

CLOTHING

- [ ] Evening outfits
- [ ] Jackets
- [ ] Outfits for each day
- [ ] Pajamas
- [ ] Socks for each day
- [ ] Undergarments for each day
- [ ] Workout clothes

SHOES

- [ ] Daytime shoes
- [ ] Evening shoes
- [ ] Workout shoes

ACCESSORIES

- [ ] Belts and/or jewelry
- [ ] Handbag(s)
- [ ] Hat
- [ ] Sunglasses

TOILETRIES

- [ ] Contact solution and case
- [ ] Contacts
- [ ] Cosmetics
- [ ] Daily facial products
- [ ] Face wipes
- [ ] Hair products
- [ ] Hairbrush
- [ ] Razor
- [ ] Toothbrush
- [ ] Toothpaste

NECESSITIES

- [ ] Chargers
- [ ] Collapsible mini umbrella
- [ ] Headphones
- [ ] Medications
- [ ] Neck pillow
- [ ] Phone
- [ ] Tablet/computer

PERFECTLY PACKED SUITCASE

We often say we have only one true skill: organizing. But lately, it seems appropriate to add "expert packers" to the list. Here are our secrets to keeping it all contained on the go.

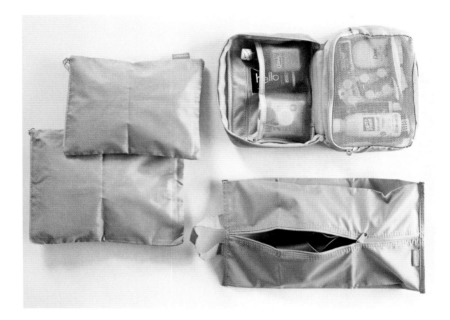

Step 1: Packing cubes are a game-changer for your suitcase, and make packing and unpacking *so* much easier. The trick is finding a set that fits what you regularly pack.

Step 2: The mesh tops are designed to ventilate your clothing, but they *also* allow you to clearly see what you have. As long as you file-fold your items so that they stand upright rather than stacking them, you can easily grab what you want without rummaging through a pile.

Step 3: For more discreet items, like undergarments and laundry, we generally prefer opaque cases. No need for TSA to literally be airing your dirty laundry.

Step 4: Specialty cases are often used to hold things like extra shoes or jewelry—but the *most* important case is certainly the one used for toiletries. We like to use toiletry bags with a lot of zippered pouches to secure their contents in place, and look for ones made of a water-resistant material in case something leaks!

[THE]
CHECKOUT LIST

DO YOU HAVE . . .

- ☐ Items from the closet?
- ☐ Items from the drawers?
- ☐ Items from the safe?
- ☐ Items from the shower?
- ☐ Jewelry?
- ☐ Phone chargers?
- ☐ Toiletries?

true story

On a recent trip to London, between the two of us, we had EIGHT SUITCASES FOR FIVE DAYS. The check-in desk at the airport asked where the rest of our party was.

WORLD
TRAVELER

What is it about foreign currency that makes it so special?
Probably that it comes in every color of the rainbow. If you
frequently travel to other countries, keep a container in your home
that holds leftover bills that you can use on future trips. Being
prepared with a tip in the PROPER currency when you check in to
a hotel is a real power move.

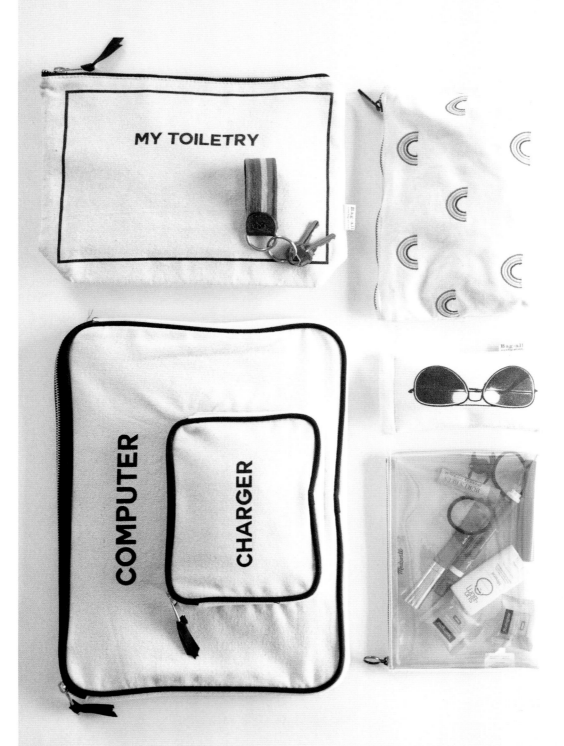

PURSE POUCHES

Whether you're prepping your handbag or an airplane carry-on, nothing helps with organization like interior pouches. And just so you can see that we practice what we preach, we emptied our own handbags to show off our systems.

1. Laptop and iPad case equipped with necessary chargers and AirPods

2. Cosmetics case

3. Sunglasses case

4. Pharmacy necessities

5. Purse snacks pouch

Purse snacks are by far the most crucial element of any handbag. You never, ever want to leave the house without at least two protein bars, a pack of almonds, and low-carb tortillas (don't knock it until you've tried it!).

true story

Sometimes we forget that we have extremely odd food habits (honestly, *most* of our habits are extremely odd), so when the low-carb purse tortillas were pulled out at a restaurant in MEXICO . . . the looks on everyone's faces were definitely warranted.

CAR
TRUNK

Organizing the trunk of your car is as simple as getting a collapsible case (The Container Store carries a few versions, or you can always buy one of the many that exist online) and packing it with the items you need most often. This particular trunk was organized with:

1. Paper towels

2. Hand towel

3. Extra pair of shoes

4. Umbrella

5. Bottles of water

6. Pen and notebook

7. Kids' car games

While organizing your own trunk, consider what you might need to have available for your kids or pets, and what types of activities require you to have some supplies on hand. Thinking through your lifestyle and its participants will help you sort out what you might want to designate specifically for your car.

POSSIBLE CAR CONTENDERS

- [ ] Blanket
- [ ] Change of clothes (for you and/or the kids)
- [ ] Dog leash
- [ ] Extra phone charger
- [ ] Hairbrush
- [ ] Hat
- [ ] Jacket
- [ ] Running shoes
- [ ] Snacks (nothing that melts)
- [ ] Sunglasses
- [ ] Sunscreen
- [ ] Yoga mat

RESORT
READY

Having a resort closet is . . . not normal. We're not going to pretend
it is. But hear us out: If you have the space and you have the items,
then why not create a special zone designed for resort wear?

Step 1: Once we designated what was actually used on beach
vacations (we are not familiar with vacations or beaches), we
corralled all the items together.

Step 2: In order to take full advantage of the space while properly
storing everything, we placed the handbags and hats on the floor of
the closet using acrylic risers. The risers allowed us to prop up the
pieces to simultaneously create functional storage and a display.

TRAVELING
BY TOUR BUS

Living in Nashville, it's no surprise we've organized our fair share of tour buses. They are all unique and have their own vibe, style, and finishes. The *most* fun thing to do on a bus (if you are a nerdy organizer, not a super-cool musician) is to tap, press, or pull on every panel, since it almost always opens to reveal a secret compartment or hidden drawers and doors. It's *also* very fun to climb in the bunks and take Boomerangs opening up the curtains. Allegedly.

Side note: You don't have to own a tour bus to follow these tips. They also apply to an RV, boat, or any other small space.

For Florida Georgia Line's **Tyler Hubbard** and his wife, Hayley, we were able to get their bus organized *before* they ever actually used it. We always jump at the opportunity to set up systems from scratch, but it also means asking a *lot* of questions. If someone has already lived in or used a space, we can tell what their habits and preferences are. But in the absence of an organizing forensic trail, we need to do our due diligence and interrogate the client.

Step 1: There's a first time for everything, and this was our first time pulling a tour bus into the store parking lot so we could make easy runs back and forth. Most of our projects don't come on wheels, so we had to seize the opportunity at hand.

Step 2: Tour buses (and other homes on wheels, such as RVs) are designed to not waste a single square inch (hence all the hidden compartments), so we wanted to make sure we had a proper plan for each cabinet. We took a stack of Post-it notes and labeled each and every space to give ourselves a road map before we started organizing.

Step 3: We began at the back of the bus, in the bathroom. Naturally, our goal was to make all the interior spaces as stunning as the interior design. The main bathroom cabinet had to hold the majority of essentials, since drawer space was limited. After accounting for towels and toilet paper, we added baskets to hold all the pharmacy and bathroom back-stock.

Step 4: Daily drawers belong in every bathroom, *especially* a bathroom on wheels. It's more practical to have items lying down and secure in drawers to avoid them tipping over in a cabinet.

true story

It might sound weird, but tour buses have carpeted drawers and shelves to keep their contents from rolling around while the bus is in motion.

Step 5: The kitchen drawers received similar treatment—most important being a dedicated coffee and tea station stocked with their favorites. Being on the road is hard, and having access to the comforts of home makes it a little easier.

IT'S OKAY TO OWN THINGS WHEN . . .

For **Thomas Rhett**'s tour bus, we wanted to set up family-friendly drawers for his wife, Lauren, and their daughters. The girls received their own drawer with sippy cups, snacks, and teethers—and Lauren was able to get a drawer of her *own* without having to share it with Thomas's shoes (see our first book for a glimpse of his collection). Another one of our favorite drawers holds all of Thomas's throat care items. Honey, tea, and cough drops are a must when you have to protect your voice.

By now, you've probably caught on that singers need a lot of hot beverages, and **Kelsea Ballerini** is no exception. Every kind of tea and coffee under the sun was organized into refillable compartments. And cold beverages (also very important, because . . . champagne) were organized into the fridge drawers.

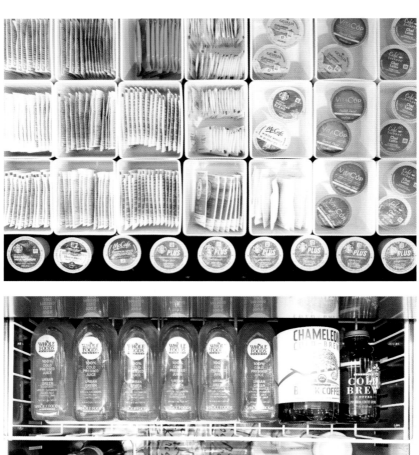

IT'S OKAY TO OWN THINGS WHEN . . .

Buses don't have spacious pantries, but we were still able to fit the main essentials in the cabinet, and a grab-and-go drawer for snacks and gum on the run!

TAKING
IT TO GO

Getting out the door in the morning can sometimes feel like climbing Mount Everest. Add kids to the mix, and it can feel more like falling off a cliff. Setting up a to-go station for your morning beverages at least helps shave a *few* minutes off your busy schedule!

Step 1: Coffee, tea, and hot chocolate were divided into their own drawers.

Step 2: We pulled the most commonly used tumblers and travel mugs out of the kitchen cabinet and placed them in their own compartment.

Step 3: Sweeteners were placed in the top drawer to keep everything in one place and complete the setup.

IT'S OKAY TO
OWN THINGS WHEN . . .

IT'S FOR YOUR WORK LIFE

We have a *lot* of sympathy for people who accumulate many things because of their profession. It's understandable that a beauty blogger would have hundreds of lipstick tubes and a basketball player would have a thousand pairs of sneakers. We don't view it as excess, we just view it as a spatial issue in need of a solution. Good thing *our* profession knows a thing or two about that.

But we aren't so innocent, either! As organizers, we have more than our fair share of leggings to work in; as business women, we have a wide array of clothing and shoes for events; as constant travelers, we have several suitcases and duffels—not to mention a purse full of paint pens, labeling supplies, phone chargers, and backup batteries! To reiterate our central belief: *Being organized doesn't mean being a minimalist.*It does not mean you need to own less.* But it *does* mean you need to treat your items, and space, appropriately and with respect.

*Unless, hypothetically, you are married to a photographer who uses very bulky equipment that takes up 90 percent of the hall closet, and even though he might need every single item for work, it's still incredibly annoying and you wish he could just use an iPhone like everyone else. But hey, at least it's stored properly.

[THE] WORKPLACE GUIDE TO GIVING YOURSELF A GREEN LIGHT

(Or, How to Know If You Should Keep an Item)

1. You use it every week. You don't just need to own it, you need "touch" access. If you need to be able to reach it at a moment's notice, you have earned your right to keep said item, whether it be in a drawer or on a shelf.

2. You might not use the *exact* same thing each week, but you use something similar and need options to do your job well. Variety is the spice of life!

3. You go through SO much of something that you need a huge amount of back-stock. We've never been afraid of back-stock, and neither should you.

4. You have multiple jobs and need multiple items. Pat yourself on the back for being the hardest worker in town and make room for everything to coexist.

5. You are building a business from home. Been there—it's tough, but not impossible. Designate an area for work and storage and try to avoid letting it seep into your living space.

IT'S OKAY TO OWN THINGS WHEN . . .

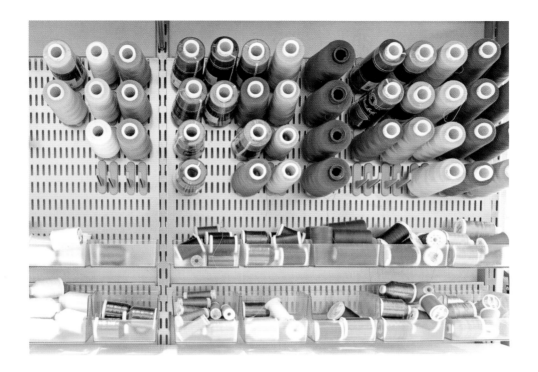

FASHION DESIGNER

Pegboards are useful in pretty much every profession, but you have to admit that spools of thread look particularly good on one. Adding extra shelves, cups, and hooks create a modular system that can grow as needed.

NURSE DURING THE WEEK, BAKER ON THE WEEKEND

This closet belongs to one of our favorite clients *ever*. Like many, she has two jobs and needed to accommodate all her items accordingly. She also was newly single, so don't think we'd miss the opportunity to add a special section of her closet devoted to dating. We told you we love a zone!

Step 1: Our goal was to set up a flow to the closet that went from weekdays to the weekend. The hanging clothes go in order from casual clothes and scrubs for during the workweek to a Friday/Saturday-night "sexy section" to church clothes for Sunday.

Step 2: With our client's second career as a home baker, we wanted to create a station that held comfy clothes to work in. We called it . . . wait for it . . . BAKE WEAR. Very pleased with ourselves.

Step 3: Since this closet used to be shared with her ex-husband, we wanted to transform it to feature her favorite colors (blush and gold), handbags, and accessories.

true story

When we found blush-colored hampers and gold label clips, we *actually* started screaming in the store.

BUSINESS
MANAGER

This is our business managers' office. Can you imagine having to deal with us all day, every day? Must be very rough. For that reason alone, we assume they need each and every item pictured here, and we just did our best to store things properly.

Step 1: In order to accommodate the large quantity of office supplies, we had an Elfa wall unit from The Container Store installed. It was important that it have enough drawer space for all the categories, but *also* a tabletop to hold printers and the postage machine.

Step 2: This is a *wall* unit, and we wanted to make the most of the wall at hand. Adding the pegboard helped us store the micro categories like clips, rubber bands, and stamps, and the hooks were able to hold scissors and tape dispensers.

Step 3: Each stack of printer paper on the top shelf directly represents the amount of paper needed to print out all of Joanna's emails. We needed to account for a lot of extra back-stock, because you never know when a 12-page email might come through!

SHOE
DESIGNER

true story

Our LA team assembled each and every one of these racks. Glad it was them and not us, because building things is *not* one of our skill sets!

IT'S OKAY TO OWN THINGS WHEN . . .

When we first posted this photo of the **APL** offices on Instagram, a lot of people thought this was someone's closet. You can imagine the collective outrage of "WHY DO THEY NEED SO MANY SHOES?!?" that followed. Good question! BECAUSE IT'S A SHOE COMPANY AND THESE ARE SAMPLES. So, yes, they need them, and they get to keep them.

SCHOOLTEACHER

Teaching is surely the most difficult job on the planet. Being responsible for a classroom of kids eight hours each day would be challenging enough, but then consider how much prep and planning goes into making those hours enjoyable and educational. Bottom line is that teachers everywhere deserve many medals for their service, but all we have to offer is help with organizing, so that will have to do.

We often talk about creating zones, but never is it more needed than in a classroom! For this one in Memphis, we set up stations for crafts, reading, and learning games so the students could help themselves. The supplies that require a bit more supervision (ahem, confetti) were stored in the closet so they could be taken out for specific projects.

IT'S OKAY TO OWN THINGS WHEN . . .

PARTY
PLANNER

There are worse ways to spend your day than organizing fun party supplies—and the **Little Miss Party** office did not disappoint! The office is *actually* an apartment, which meant the closets were for hanging clothes—not hanging packs of balloons. That is, until we got there.

Step 1: The shelving unit was already living in the closet, so we wanted to put it to good use and maximize as much vertical space as possible. If things are simply piled on the shelves, it doesn't do you *or* them any good. Especially when you consider how delicate paper products can be.

Step 2: There is nothing more satisfying than getting a perfect fit, and this combination of drawers and acrylic holders fit the shelf without an inch to spare. We were able to separate all the small categories into their own clear compartments to make packing up for parties that much easier. To take advantage of the hanging rod, we used hooks normally reserved for handbags and placed packs of lanterns and Mylar balloons instead.

Step 3: You can't organize an office for partying without throwing a little party at the end. We put all those "POP FIZZ CLINK" cups to good use and had a champagne toast!

IT'S OKAY TO OWN THINGS WHEN . . .

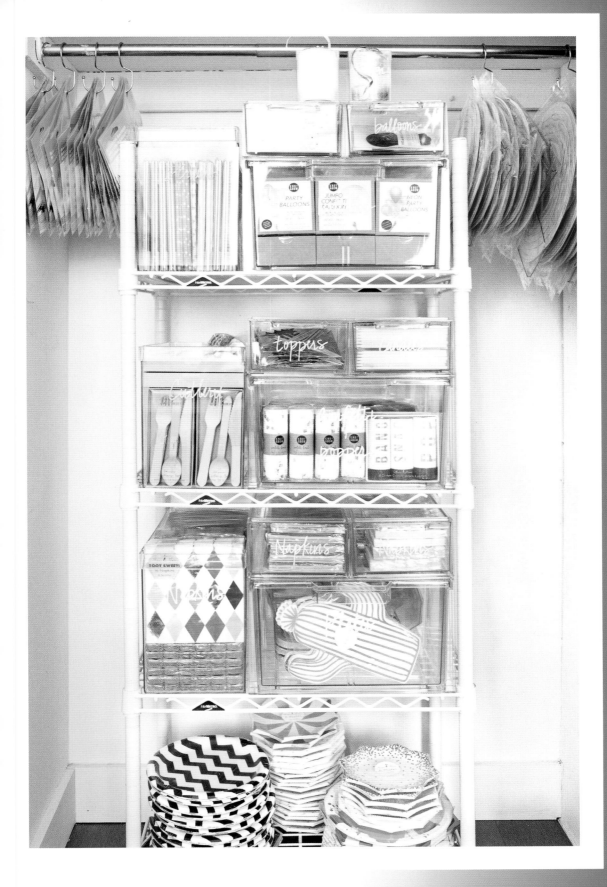

DESIGNER
AND
SHOP OWNER

Our best friend Leah, from **Love & Lion**, works out of her home office. And while the walls and desktop are so perfectly curated, she had piles of inventory everywhere. But when you run an online shop, you can't cut *down* on inventory. The best you can do is find a better way to store everything before you lose your child under a pile of T-shirts.

Step 1: The merchandise was sorted into the core categories: T-shirts, temporary tattoos, totes, and wrapping paper (really wish there was another word for wrapping paper that started with a "T," but what can you do).

Step 2: We corralled all the shipping supplies onto the top shelf to make packing orders that much easier.

Step 3: All the wrapped gift boxes (and Harry Potter glasses) are actually props used for fairs and vendor events, so we set them aside and put them into a self-contained basket.

true story

Rolls of wrapping paper are not the easiest things to store . . . so we ended up using a combination of magazine holders and wastebaskets. There's *always* a solution, but some require unconventional thinking.

YOUTUBE
STUDIO

This was our very first time organizing a YouTube studio, and we wanted to knock it out of the park for **Shay Mitchell**. You'd think it wouldn't be *that* complicated, but there was so much equipment we had never seen before. We had to keep texting photos to Clea's husband, John, asking him to identify cables and cameras. And that was before we got to all the beauty and hair products! There was a lot of phoning a friend with this project!

Step 1: The studio was divided into three zones: beauty and styling products, electronic and fitness equipment, and cameras and lights.

Step 2: Once we realized the difference between cables that *charge* and cables that *transmit* information . . . well, let's just say we felt *quite* pleased with ourselves. As if we had cracked a secret intel code. All the cables were masterfully divided into their own bins so that any poor soul who came after us wouldn't get them mixed up.

Step 3: For the most-used beauty products—like lip glosses and hair sprays—we set up a combination of makeup caddies and turntables. Back-stock and bulky products went into the drawers below!

RETAIL OFFICE

We love having **Kristin Cavallari** in Nashville and were *very* excited when she opened her boutique, **Uncommon James**, downtown. But we were probably even more excited to organize her offices.

Step 1: Kristin loves a color palette, and we are here for it. Blush, white, and gold, you say? Consider it done. We loaded up on pink paper supplies and even sourced pink vinyl for custom Cricut labels (our favorite being the "forgot something?" tray next to the printer).

Step 2: No office is complete without snacks, and we wanted the setup to match the aesthetic of the office. We color coordinated the snacks with the surroundings, and hand-stacked them à la Khloé Kardashian.

Step 3: Office celebrations call for a party drawer (yes, we labeled that, too!), and now these balloons, candles, and straws are ready for a good time.

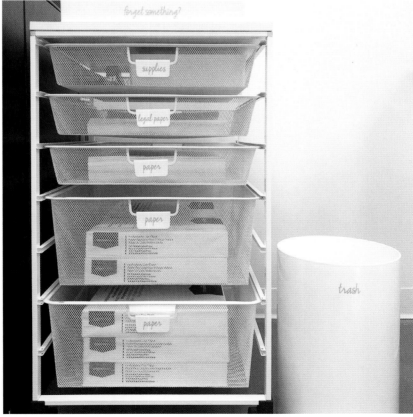

BASKETBALL PLAYER

Organizing **Dwyane Wade**'s basketball shoes was a labor of love. We had several projects going on throughout the house, but when we passed by the sneaker closet . . . how could we *not* take every single shoe down and start from scratch? It would be a crime against humanity. Not only does Dwyane ACTUALLY USE them (he walks in several times throughout the day and picks a pair for practice, games, etc.), but they are all his personal brand, so he needs to show off the variety of colors and styles. Having them organized and easy to navigate was mission critical.

Step 1: Organizing all these shoes actually turned into a mathematical equation. There could be X many across each shelf, and X many in each column. So in order to prevent a Rubik's Cube situation, we actually *counted* each of the pairs and created a road map for putting the collection back together.

true story

Organizing basketball shoes is effective exercise. Each shoe feels like a five-pound barbell, and we clocked eight miles in *one* day going up and down the ladder.

Step 2: In addition to all the pairs on the shelf, there were also boxes of unpacked shoes that needed to be integrated with the rest. We accounted for those and worked them into the equation, too.

Step 3: With the constant arrival of new styles, we made sure to leave an open area on the back wall to accommodate additional pairs. Remember, having room to grow is an integral part of our process. Once you cross 80 percent capacity, you run the risk of losing control of your space.

BEAUTY BLOGGER

Normally, when someone owns more than one hundred lip liners, we suggest paring them down. There's no way they use all of them, right?! But when this someone is a beauty blogger, that's another story. **Karen Gonzalez** from iluvsarahii doesn't just own a lot of makeup—her entire career revolves around it. Our ultimate goal was to create a space that highlights her passion for beauty and simplifies her everyday work routine.

Step 1: We divided the studio into a zone for cosmetics and a separate zone for hair and beauty products.

Step 2: Makeup collections require a lot of categorization, so we built a configuration that would store and separate all the face, cheek, lip, and eye products.

Step 3: We designated the closet shelves for skincare, hair products, and accessories. Turntables are a perfect way to store sprays and serums, since they keep the products upright and accessible!

Step 4: The hanging rod in the closet keeps all the fabric and drop cloths used for prop styling on shoots. Uniform wire hangers help maximize space and protect the delicate fabric.

IT'S OKAY TO
OWN THINGS WHEN . . .

YOU
HAVE
KIDS

If you have children, are planning to have children, or have ever spent time with children, you have probably realized by now that kids = many (sometimes many, many, many) things. And while we don't want you to feel guilty for having toys and craft supplies in your house, it's still critical that you follow our rules so that your home doesn't turn into a toy store.

In our first book, we shared some of the ways we declutter our *own* homes—like running through the house with garbage bags the second our kids leave for school and donating everything not nailed down to the floors. Well, we didn't consider that by the time the book was released, our kids would be able to READ. Our children were *not* amused, to say the least. But it was also a good opportunity to remind them that when they leave their toys, clothes, games, puzzles, and stuffed animals on the floor, it tells others that they don't value those items. And what's the point of keeping something you don't value? This is all to say, we are *very* fun moms. But it's *also* to say that it's perfectly fine to own the aforementioned toys and games, providing they are properly contained and organized. No one wants their living room to turn into a breeding ground for puzzle parts.

TIPS ON
KID CLUTTER

1. **If it's broken:** It goes in the trash. Immediately. You will not fix it, you can't donate it, and your best friend's daughter doesn't want a broken toy!

2. **If it's missing a part:** See above.

3. **If they've outgrown it:** You can either (a) hold on to it for your next child, or (b) pass it on to a friend's appropriately aged child.

4. **If they love it but you don't:** They get to keep it. . . . Yes, it's your home, but it's their childhood. The second they lose interest, however, it's fair game. Grab that donation bag!

5. **If it's too special to part with:** You never, *ever* need to get rid of things that are special to you. Ever! But it's imperative you store these items in a way that honors their importance. Whether it's their first blanket, their childhood favorite toy, or a graduation cap and gown, it should all be binned up and labeled. Otherwise, you are just letting your most sentimental items gather dust and will eventually lose track of where they are.

When it comes to kids, there are a whole host of reasons people might own more things than someone else. Everyone has different circumstances, space constraints, preferences, and sheer *number* of children. Our goal is to create storage solutions for these items that allow others to live unencumbered and without guilt.

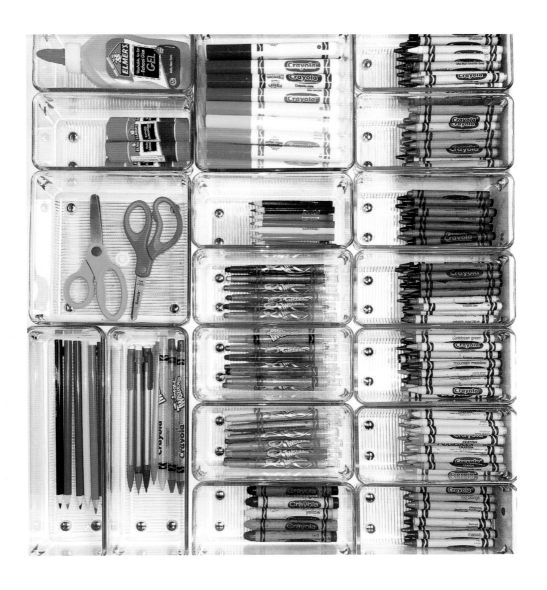

RAINBOW
TWINS

For those of you who have never heard the term "rainbow baby," or in this case, "rainbow TWINS," it refers to a baby (or babies) born after losing a baby to miscarriage, infant loss, or other tragic circumstance. So you can imagine how seriously we took this organizing challenge. We had two main goals: (1) set up systems to house the ENORMOUS amount of baby supplies needed for twins, and (2) bring happiness and joy to the nursery. This room was previously meant for the baby who was lost, so it was a difficult space for the parents to tackle on their own.

Step 1: We needed to add extra storage opportunities to hold ALL. THE. DIAPERS. Newborn twins need about 600 diapers in the first month. That is not a typo: 6-0-0. And when you have twins to change, you need diapers at the ready, since you have only two hands (is anyone else getting stressed out just thinking about this?). So we added an over-the-door rack to store easily accessible back-stock of diapers, wipes, and lotions.

Step 2: The top drawers in the changing table were the perfect spot to hold the front-stock of diaper supplies.

Step 3: All the baby clothes were sifted and sorted into piles according to age. And then . . . of course we lined them up in two rainbows. It would be organizing malpractice to let that moment pass us by! Plus, it helped us achieve both our goals at once. Clothes in larger sizes they would grow into, we placed in labeled baskets on the top shelf.

Step 4: To store all the foldable items, accessories, and hair bows, we added two carts with drawers.

Step 5: We wanted to highlight the handmade bookcase on page 143 that was made by our client's father. It's positioned in the middle of the room and adds one extra rainbow of toys and books.

DEALING WITH DIAPER CHANGES

You don't have to have twins to need a LOT of diapers. New parents are often overwhelmed (parents in *general* are often overwhelmed), and middle-of-the-night diaper changes do not help with anxiety levels. So when we set up a changing table, we try to bring ourselves back to the newborn years and remember what we urgently needed at three a.m. while having one hand on the baby, one hand in the drawer, one eye open, and zero lights to help the cause.

Step 1: The diapers were all separated by size, and the drawer was filled with the size that currently fit the baby.

Step 2: Wipes and *extra* wipes were added. When it comes to a newborn, you can never have too many wipes on hand, and it's easy to line the back of the drawer with the surplus.

Step 3: All the items that might be helpful in a pinch were organized into the remaining compartments: diaper cream, gas relief, and swaddles for comfort.

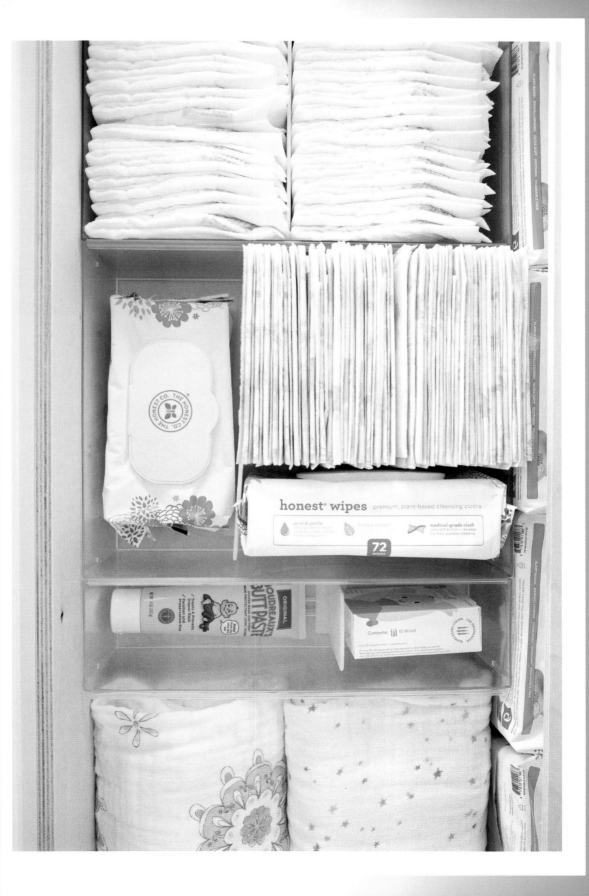

FEEDING
A NEWBORN

Of course **Lauren Conrad** makes her own baby food. We genuinely thought these contraptions were some kind of cappuccino maker and coffee pot until she explained they were used to prepare homemade baby food. We don't know much about the preparation, but we were happy to organize all the supplies in the kitchen cabinet!

Step 1: Baby appliances (not for coffee) were moved to the bottom shelf for easy access.

Step 2: The coordinating appliance supplies, and small items like pacifiers and bottle parts, were organized into adjacent stackable drawers.

Step 3: The number of baby bottle washes rivals the number of diaper changes, so we lined up the soap back-stock on the top shelf next to the body and hand soaps.

EXPECTING A BABY GIRL

We wanted to accomplish a few things with **Mindy Kaling**'s nursery closet. First and foremost, the goal was to unpack, unbox, and store all the incoming items. But we *really* wanted to create a setup that was whimsical, bright, and fitting for a little girl. Mindy is known for her sense of color and style, and every room in the house is more beautiful than the next. So naturally the nursery had to be just as beautiful as its surroundings.

Step 1: First-time pregnancy + a baby girl = a lot of tiny pink items. So our first order of business was to separate out all the pink pieces to highlight them in the closet.

Step 2: The onesies, baby socks, and burp cloths were folded into drawers, and the dresses and coats were put on hangers (who doesn't want to look at a little ombré faux fur?).

Step 3: For the shelves, we carefully lined up the shoes (there is nothing, *nothing* more fun than shopping for baby shoes) in shades of pink, folded bedding and sheet sets, and displayed accessories and books.

Step 4: Knowing that new babies come with new memories, we added sentimental boxes (and a pop of bright blue!) so that Mindy could collect anything that felt special.

KIDS WHO LIKE TO MAKE A MESS

If you have kids who enjoy messy art, having paint and slime supplies is probably a given. But messy art doesn't have to mean a messy house. By setting up a station, you can contain the chaos to a single location so it doesn't seep into the rest of your home. Some parents are easygoing enough to allow an art station in the playroom or kitchen cabinets—personally, we know nothing about an easygoing existence and prefer a setup in the garage (which honestly feels generous).

Step 1: All messy art supplies were isolated into their own bins—they don't play well with others, and therefore get no other bin roommates.

Step 2: Drop cloths, Play-Doh tools, paintbrushes, and any coordinating supplies were organized separately and kept in close proximity.

Step 3: After checking, double-checking, and triple-checking whether the kids were allowed to have access to the items (so, so very brave), we placed everything within reach, keeping the heaviest items at the bottom.

KIDS WHO
CRAFT

Crafting is the first cousin of messy art, so they *can* overlap. Just
remain vigilant, stick to your stations, and don't be afraid to separate
pipe cleaners and pom-poms from glitter and glue. Also, don't be
afraid to ban glitter from your home entirely . . . It's been known to
happen. Sorry not sorry, kids.

Step 1: The craft supplies were separated into two groups: "better in a canister" and "better in a drawer." There's no right or wrong answer, but if you have different storage options, it's best to use everything available. In this case, canisters were utilized for larger groupings (see page 155), and smaller pieces were placed in drawers.

Step 2: All the bits were organized with similar items. For instance, tape, clips, and stickers all attach and adhere, so they were placed together.

KIDS WITH SCARY FOOD ALLERGIES

Severe food allergies are a parent's worst nightmare. Every nutrition label feels like it has a skull and crossbones on it instead of a list of ingredients. And if you have multiple children with different dietary restrictions, it becomes necessary to have more food on hand than you otherwise would. This particular pantry and fridge might be one of the most high-pressure projects we've ever undertaken. . . . It's not every day that organizing feels like life or death, but in this case, it's an accurate description.

Step 1: All the pantry allergens (anything with nuts or dairy) were corralled and moved to a separate area of the kitchen for organizing.

Step 2: Safe snacks were organized into bins that the whole family could access, while the skull-and-crossbones snacks were placed in a bin on the top shelf. You can't see it in this image, but we even labeled it "DANGER ZONE" to avoid any possible mix-up (not on our watch)!

Step 3: The fridge was even scarier than the pantry, due to the closer proximity of the items and the *additional* allergens (beef and pork), so clearly a danger zone was needed here, too. We divided the fridge in half and used bins for every food item (even inside the drawers) in case anything leaked or dripped.

Step 4: The drawers were carefully labeled with each child's name to avoid any cross-contamination (labeling has never felt more serious).

IT'S OKAY TO OWN THINGS WHEN . . .

NINE KIDS

Remember how we mentioned that we constantly have to defend our clients from comments like, "Who needs that many bottles of soap??" This is a prime example of a family who really (*really*) needs that many bottles of soap. In fact, they need that many of every item they own, because they have nine children! NINE! And not a single set of twins, stepchildren, or half siblings. We've seen it with our own eyes and met every single one of them, but it's still hard to fathom. So, yes, they get to keep anything that helps their family function, because it can't be easy.

Step 1: Of the nine kids, there are six who are currently in school and need to make a mad dash out the door on weekdays. The laundry room has turned into a hub for their morning routine, so we set up a station for them to brush their teeth, take their vitamins, and grab their lunch boxes.

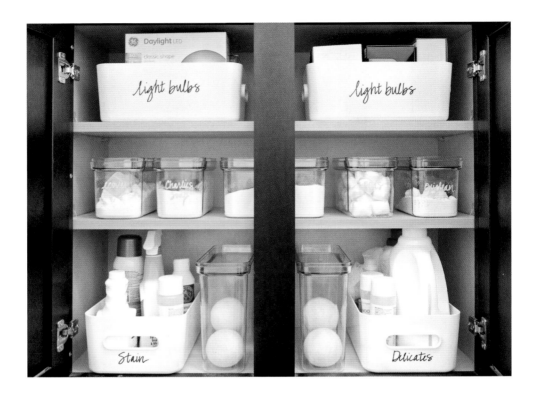

Step 2: We organized the rest of the laundry room for the actual 12,000 loads of laundry that occur on a daily basis. Some of the kids have skin sensitivities, so we made sure to use different canisters for specialty detergents.

Step 3: All that soap had to go *somewhere,* so we added extra storage units to the walls. Again, this looks like a lot of back-stock until you consider how many hands, and dishes, need constant washing.

SCHOOL-AGE KIDS

If newborns are synonymous with diaper changes, then kids in elementary school are synonymous with paper. The. Endless. Amount. Of. Paper. They come home with backpacks full of art projects, spelling tests, drawing doodles, and scraps of something they started but abandoned yet is still somehow considered special and worthy of keeping. And yes, some of it certainly *is* worthy. But not all of it. Try to apply your most objective voice of reason when deciding what to keep and what to toss (feeling very nervous about our kids reading this section).

Step 1: The piles of paper were sorted into schoolwork, artwork, art projects, and memories. It's important to use storage boxes that actually fit the items you intend to store, so one size accommodates paper and the other accommodates bulky projects or larger sentimental items.

Step 2: Coloring doesn't happen only at school! All the crayons, markers, and colored pencils were organized into colorful boxes for a rainbow effect.

Step 3: School supplies and notebooks were kept on top of the desk for easy access, while less-used items like sticker sheets and coloring books were placed in the drawers.

KIDS
WHO PLAY
SPORTS

This is a topic we know little about, since athleticism doesn't run in either of our families. . . . But we *have* picked up a few tips and tricks here and there, so hopefully we can help you apply them to your space, too. The main thing we've learned is that having kids who play multiple sports involving different teams, leagues, and tournaments is a major commitment. Not just in energy and time (although hats off to all you incredibly involved parents!), but also in the amount of real estate you give up to house all the required equipment and gear. Coaches should honestly send home disclaimer forms warning how much space you will have to forgo for each sport.

Step 1: All sports equipment was sorted (and yes, we took extra pleasure in considering lightsabers as a category) and divided into zones.

Step 2: Baseball was the most prominent sport, so the bats, balls, and mitts received the most devoted storage (and the utility rack normally reserved for mops and brooms worked so perfectly with the baseball bats!).

Step 3: Additional gear and outdoor items were stored in adjacent drawers.

IT'S OKAY TO OWN THINGS WHEN . . .

If you opt for an indoor setup instead of the garage, consider a cubby system like the one we implemented here. All the bulky items are in concealed baskets, and the shelves contain everything from golf balls to shin guards. And if each team requires different jerseys or footwear, just remember to label them as such!

IT'S OKAY TO OWN THINGS WHEN . . .

IT'S OKAY TO
OWN THINGS WHEN . . .

YOU
HAVE
PETS

O ur pets are kids, too, right? We love them like children, we treat them like members of the family, and yes, they, *too,* need an abundance of things on any given day. And we owe it to them to give them all those things. After all, they love us unconditionally, never explicitly ask us to buy them a *single* thing, and bring home ZERO ART PROJECTS. They don't even talk back! We should all have a house full of cats or a farm with dogs. They are truly the unsung heroes of the household.

A COUPLE
OF CATS

Cats are animals after our own hearts . . . They are social only when it pleases them, their hobbies include bathing and people-watching, and they're fine when their family leaves for a few days. The other great thing about cats is that they leave a smaller footprint (literally) than dogs, so the storage systems are much less of an undertaking.

Step 1: Truthfully, this cat did *not* like Joanna (apparently there was a squabble while organizing the master closet, from which neither of them recovered). We all agreed to disagree, so the first order of business was to separate the two and send them to their respective corners.

Step 2: Look how fun all these little cat bits and bobbles are! We took our time separating grooming items, tiny toys, and food bowls.

Step 3: While the litter supplies went in the cabinets, we kept feeding supplies down in the drawer so it was less cumbersome to prepare meals.

FURRY
FAMILY

For many animal lovers, one just isn't enough. But it also means that twice the amount of supplies are needed. In order to keep your home from turning into a boarding kennel, it's important to add storage solutions before things get out of hand. In this home, we created a zone in the garage to hold the various beds, litter, and grooming supplies. For the smaller items like toys and dress-up clothes (cat costumes are a real thing), we set up stackable bins and turntables on the top shelf.

DOGS ARE A (HU)MAN'S BEST FRIEND

Need we remind you that dogs love you unconditionally? Who else can you even say that about? Your mother? Sure . . . she might, but doesn't she *also* call you to say she saw your Instagram stories from your trip to London and counted how many drinks you had? We love our mothers. So much. But dogs can't call or count, and that generates a lot of goodwill in our book.

Step 1: Many people store their pet supplies in the laundry room. In fact, the laundry room turns into a "household" room of sorts, so everything from utility items to cleaning supplies to dog food ends up being stored there. Our first order of business was to separate the categories into bins and then prioritize the shelves based on usage. *Obviously* their dog received the most critical real estate. But thankfully, since the shelving had doors and dogs don't have thumbs, there won't be a treat heist.

Step 2: Within the pet-land zone, we reordered the bins to give easier access to the most-used items like food and treats. The costumes— while very cute—were less of a priority, and moved up a shelf.

For a much larger dog, like **Laura Dern**'s, we opted for heavy-duty bins to store heavy-duty items. Everything from the size of the leash to the size of the bone gets exponentially larger, so we wanted to ensure we left enough room for additional items. The categories are similar to the dog zone on page 176 (wet food, dry food, grooming, walking, and treats), but not a single costume in sight. We're going to have to send Jamal something to wear for Halloween this year!

This laundry room was designed with built-in dog crates, so we wanted to keep the countertop as clean and crisp as the rest of the room. Food and treats were stored in corner canisters, and the center tray held a scent station to keep the room smelling dog-free.

WHEN A DOG
IS KIND
OF A BIG DEAL

We've worked with a lot of celebrities, but have any been as important as **Doug the Pug**? It's not every day you get to experience the Pug Life firsthand. Doug is gracious, warm, *very* cuddly, and probably the least demanding of any client we've worked with thus far. He literally didn't bark once.

When we started the project, we surveyed the mountains of clothing (Doug wears a children's size 3T, BTW) and realized we needed to install a proper closet system to organize all the categories. The Container Store came to our collective rescue and designed a custom Elfa system to go along the entire wall.

Step 1: We sorted and sorted and sorted some more. Themes played a big part in the process, since Doug's owners need to be able to easily find a pizza costume (food drawer), or a pumpkin costume (Halloween drawer), or a flower lei (luau drawer).

Step 2: For Doug's specialty or couture pieces (yes, that is correct— what else was he supposed to wear to the royal wedding?), we hung them on the rack above to avoid folding.

Step 3: Besides being an Internet sensation, Doug is a merchandise mogul. So we obviously had to fill his closet showcasing his collection.

Step 4: You know we love a display wall, and this closet was no exception. The little boots, moccasins, and sneakers were lined up neatly on the shelves, and the sunglasses collection (pretty impressive for a pug!) were arranged in rainbow order.

misc. clothes

Step 5: The foldable accessories like handkerchiefs and bow ties were organized in the drawers directly below.

A . . .
SQUIRREL?

Your guess is as good as ours. . . . We just organize what we're told to. And we were told to create this setup for a special furry friend. Mission accomplished.

Step 1: After careful consideration of the squirrel's living habits and preferences, we concluded that zones don't matter . . . because it's a squirrel.

Step 2: Mixed nuts and shelled nuts were divided into labeled canisters, and back-stock went into the basket above.

IT'S OKAY TO
OWN THINGS WHEN . . .

YOU LOVE TO CELE-BRATE

S ome people like to celebrate, and some like to be celebrated. Just like how some people like to *give* presents, and some people like to *receive* presents. (Refer back to our personality types and guess which buckets we fall in.) But for those who like to do the celebrating, we see you, and will gladly organize all your serving dishes, cutlery, and wrapping paper.

GREAT AT GIFTING

Thank goodness gift-givers exist. It makes us gift-receivers feel better knowing there was genuine enjoyment while picking out the right hostess gift or perfect party favor. We would never want to rob you of that happiness, so we will happily squeal with excitement whenever you hand over a gift bag tied with a bow.

Step 1: All the gifts were removed from the shelves and categorized by occasion: housewarming, holiday, kids, and extras.

Step 2: The majority of the items were for home and hostess, so we kept those down low, and moved the kids' items to higher shelves to keep them out of reach and out of sight.

Step 3: The cabinet doors were designed to hold rolls of wrapping paper, so naturally we wanted to help them fulfill their destiny. And then we lined up all the rolls in rainbow order to help fulfill *our* destiny.

TIPS FOR GROWING
YOUR GIFT COLLECTION

1. Your child receives a gift that requires batteries, makes noise, or contains glitter: Swipe it when they aren't looking and put it in the regift pile.

2. You receive a gift box and want only 50 percent of the contents: Put the other 50 percent to good use and give them as future gifts.

3. Your father buys you amethyst earrings every year and you don't have the heart to tell him that you hate purple even though it's your birthstone. . . . Surely someone else would love them.

4. You find a gift you love to give (candle, book, etc.): Buy multiples so you are never empty-handed.

5. If you can't return it and don't like it, then don't keep it! Gifting it to someone else is a much better alternative.

IT'S OKAY TO OWN THINGS WHEN . . .

Gift-givers need a lot of wrapping supplies. You can't just show up
to a dinner or birthday party holding an unwrapped scented candle.
For this particular setup, we took over a cabinet to hold all the tissue,
tinsel, and toppers. Tissue paper is often unruly to store, so try not
to worry about getting it to look perfect. Getting it contained (and
organized by color) is good enough!

Some gift wrap stations are fancier than others. If you
have the space and want to create a focal point, hang frames with
removable rods to hold ribbon and rolls. It certainly makes wrapping
a gift that much more fun!

START
CHRISTMAS
IN OCTOBER

You know those people who complain about Christmas music starting before December 1? Let's just say we are not those people. You give us a pile of red and green gift tags, and we will happily sort them while singing "Jingle Bells" ANY TIME of year.

Check out this Christmas goodie drawer full of decorations and small gifts. We added the drawer inserts to keep the categories separated, but made sure to leave enough room in the drawer so that new items could be added.

IT'S OKAY TO OWN THINGS WHEN . . .

INDOOR
AND
OUTDOOR
ENTERTAINING

While organizing **Whitney Port**'s entertaining supplies, we noticed two things: (1) She had enough items to warrant their own closet, and (2) many of the pieces were meant to be used outdoors. It *is* LA, after all, and poolside entertaining is taken very seriously.

Step 1: The items were separated into indoor and outdoor categories, along with frequency of use.

Step 2: Outdoor cutlery and serving pieces were organized into their own divided caddies so they could be easily transported to the dining table outside.

Step 3: Less-used items, like teacups and serving bowls, were placed on the back wall so that they didn't take up prime real estate. We needed to leave plenty of room for those pineapple tumblers!

IT'S OKAY TO OWN THINGS WHEN . . .

With a more simplified setup, you can avoid using storage containers altogether and just optimize the shelves by lining up all the items by category. Entertaining items are extra bulky, so it's just important to space them out accordingly!

FAMILY
FOOTBALL
RIVALRY

We are *not* trying to get in between **Thomas Rhett** and **Lauren Akins** when it comes to football. To be honest, we wouldn't get between *strangers* when it comes to football. It's a sport, right? Unclear if it's the kicking one or the catching one, but it appears to be very popular. And from all our time in the Akins household, we know they take it VERY SERIOUSLY. Thomas is a Georgia Bulldogs fan, and Lauren is strictly Tennessee Volunteers. Which is FINE, since we have zero skin in the game and just aim to please.

Step 1: We carefully divided all the supplies into his and hers categories as though we were defusing a bomb. We were willing to do our part to ensure football Sunday remained fun and uncomplicated!

Step 2: For guests who are not fiercely divided by team loyalty, we arranged plenty of neutral cups (and back-stock cups!) at the bar (see the following page). Yes, we know they are red, which *could* lean Georgia, but we're going to stay out of it.

IT'S OKAY TO OWN THINGS WHEN . . .

For serious sports fans who attend games or host watch parties at home, we set up stations to house all the jerseys, swag, and scarves. There's even a holiday section to allow for team spirit *and* Santa spirit.

And then there are people who like to have everyone over to watch the [fill in the blank] game. It doesn't matter which sport or which team is playing, as long as the TV is on and beer is available. For situations like these, we like to set up a Koozie station that can be transported outside as needed. When guests arrive, they can grab a beer and get a Koozie to keep it cold!

And if cold beverages require a straw, just add an extra compartment! We accommodate all drinks without judgment.

true story

A few years ago, we had no idea what a Koozie was. . . . We thought it was that knitted thing that went over a teapot. Cut to a few years later, and now we know it's a sport fan's staple.

A NAPKIN FOR EVERY OCCASION

Some people might see a closet full of napkins and panic. Not us. Shelves and shelves of linens in different colors and prints are quite literally the dream. And the challenge of coming up with a storage solution is what nerdy organizers live for.

Step 1: You know what is similarly sized to a folded napkin? A woman's shoe. Shockingly accurate dimensions, and very helpful when sourcing product. We ended up using a combination of stacking shoe dividers and clear shoe boxes to store all the varieties.

Step 2: We created a color gradient because do *not* threaten us with a good time!

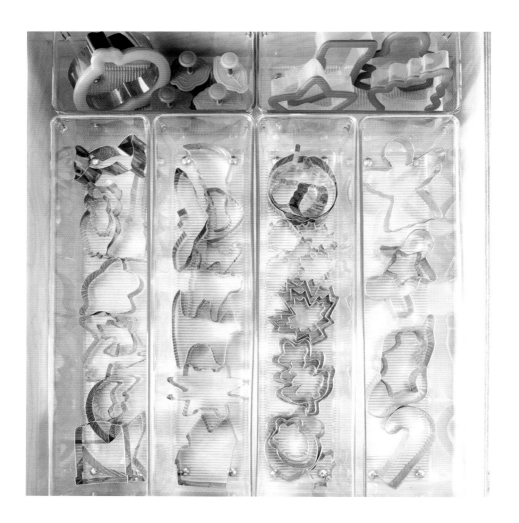

SERIOUS
CELEBRATORS

We don't even know how to cook, let alone bake, but we love a cookie
cutter collection and will happily sort and categorize the shapes all
day long. Of course we categorized by holiday *and* season so we
could organize everything in calendar order. Yes, we are crazy.

IT'S OKAY TO OWN THINGS WHEN . . .

Not everyone is season specific—sometimes it's more about birthdays and everyday gatherings. For this drawer, we separated and organized the straws from the toothpicks, and the candles from the cutlery.

IT'S OKAY TO
OWN THINGS WHEN . . .

IT
SERVES A
PURPOSE

This section isn't glamorous, but that's the point. Remember the toilet plunger we referenced at the beginning? We all NEED toilet plungers. And we also need laundry detergent, rags, and lightbulbs. These things aren't fun, but you know what's also not fun? Living without laundry detergent, rags, and lightbulbs. So we are here to say that if it solves a problem and serves a useful function, then by all means, stock up. There are plenty of ways to store and organize all these items, and owning a decent supply is generally part of having a well-stocked household, so you don't overbuy.

true story

This is **Eva Chen**'s kitchen, and when she saw this picture on Instagram, she said, "Why does this person need so much vinegar???" And then she realized it was *her* vinegar.

COMPULSIVE CLEANER

We said it before, and we will say it again: Cleaning counts as cardio. Why *not* get the dual benefit of exercise and a clean house? Yoga class won't get the dishes done, and push-ups won't tidy the playroom!

Step 1: After assessing the closet storage options, it was clear that additional options were needed. We installed our MVP (most valuable product); an over-the-door unit.

Step 2: Once the baskets were loaded up with sprays, rags, and dusting cloths, we used the leftover space to store a roll of paper towels and a roll of trash bags. Having all your cleaning supplies conveniently located makes cleaning up that much easier.

We often end up storing the majority of cleaning products under the kitchen sink, since it's the one spot *every* home has, regardless of size. In order to optimize every inch, we use stackable bins to take advantage of the cabinet height (the bottom bin is actually a sliding drawer unit so that items remain accessible without having to take the top bin off), and we line up supplies down the middle where the pipes are located.

Another space we often take over for cleaning products is a laundry room cabinet. And since laundry rooms are generally not used exclusively for laundry, we frequently call them "household rooms"—because yes, we label *all* things even if it's just a label we create mentally. Once you relabel a space, other items start to inherently make more sense when stored there. This cabinet might have started off with laundry detergent, but with the addition of sprays and wipes, it now serves to clean the entire house.

IT'S OKAY TO OWN THINGS WHEN . . .

In this household cabinet, laundry supplies are designed to be readily accessible, but the top shelves were repurposed to store lightbulbs. If you get too focused on a room being meant to hold specific things, you end up not having room for something else. But once you reframe the context of the room, then soaps, sprays, and lightbulbs can most definitely live together.

HANDY
AT HOME

Admittedly, we know *nothing* about tools. We don't know how to use them, we don't know what they are all called, and it's not high on our list to figure either of these things out. So . . . when we organize tool collections, we default to what we *do* know: lining things up according to the rainbow.

Step 1: All the loose thingamabobs were spread out on the floor and grouped with . . . similar-looking thingamabobs.

Step 2: Once we identified what we wanted to hang on the pegboard versus store in the drawers, we attached enough hooks, cups, and ledges to accommodate everything.

Step 3: THANKFULLY, the grouped thingamabobs formed the entire color spectrum, so we were able to line up everything according to the rainbow. We figured since the client had *bought* every color of the rainbow, they would want us to make the most of the situation.

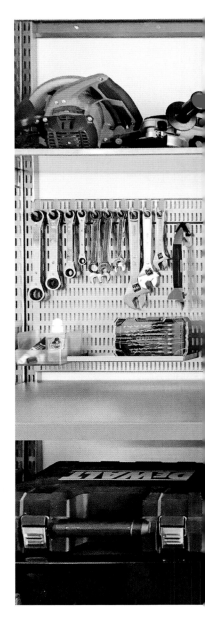

IT'S OKAY TO OWN THINGS WHEN . . .

IT SERVES A PURPOSE

Sometimes a simple solution is the best solution. And since we are *quite* clear that this is not our strongest area of expertise, storing all the basic tools together in accessible bins felt like the best approach.

Utility items are the first cousin of tools, but much more in our comfort zone. Dividing various adhesives and battery types into compartments is actually pretty therapeutic. As for the nails and screws, while it's edging into tool territory, you don't need to know how to use them to instinctively know they should be separated.

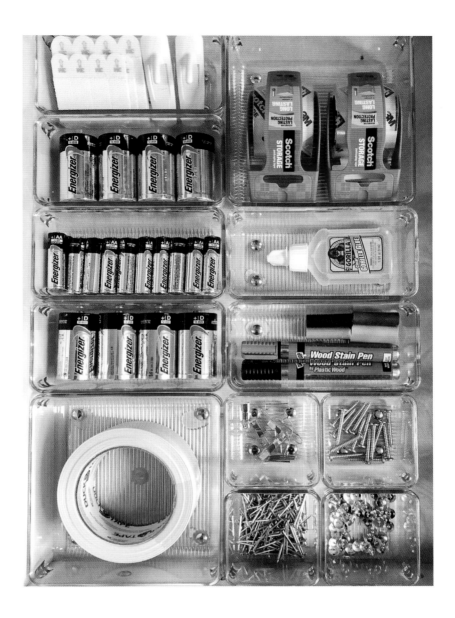

true story

Joanna is TERRIFIED of batteries. Specifically
battery *acid*, but she's so convinced that every
battery is about to spontaneously combust that
she refuses to organize them and passes that
part of the project to someone else.

HOUSEHOLD BACK-STOCK

We all need a spot in the home that holds the extra items we can't live without. Whether it's toilet paper and paper towels or diapers and cold medicine, you do *not* want to have to go to the store at eleven p.m. when you realize you're out of said item. For **Eva Chen**, we were tasked with getting her back-stock closet under control, because even though she *had* all the necessities stocked, it was impossible to find anything.

Step 1: We took over the entire living room and hallway in order to organize the closet contents. While everything was piled up in groups on the floor, we measured and wiped down the shelves.

Step 2: The closet has a decent amount of shelf space, but not all of it is easily accessible. When setting up the bin configuration, we made sure to earmark the ones obscured by the doorway for the least-used items, and the ones down the center for the most frequently used items.

Step 3: The bins were carefully loaded with the contents to ensure that we could stack the majority of them. This is a New York City apartment so using all the available space was an even bigger priority than usual!

ALWAYS PREPARED WITH A PEN

We're not suggesting that you will need to make a midnight run because you can't find a pen, but . . . when you want one and can't find any, it's very annoying. And we have all been guilty of signing something with a washable marker because it's the only thing around. That's why it's always helpful to have a section devoted to basic office supplies. Using these stackable drawers, we fit nine essential categories onto a single cabinet shelf.

The benefit of this setup is that the space limitations in each drawer keep you from overbuying supplies. Everyone needs pens, but no one needs more than a single drawer full. Nor does any one person need more than three staplers. Leave room for other items.

IT'S OKAY TO OWN THINGS WHEN . . .

WINTRY WEATHER

People in California might look at this picture and think it's absurd to give so much closet real estate to all-weather boots. So let us assure you, there are many places in the country that require ALL sorts of weather gear, and they need to be readily accessible. Setting up this winter-weather zone makes it easier to get out the door in the morning and keeps piles of scarves from accumulating on the floor.

IT'S OKAY TO
OWN THINGS WHEN . . .

IT
MAKES
YOU
HAPPY

If you read only one section of this whole book, we hope it's this one. We can make all sorts of cases for why people need to own all sorts of things, but the best defense for owning something is that it makes you happy. Or it "sparks joy," to borrow a phrase from Marie Kondo. Yes, it's appropriate to own things for your kids, your work, and all the various aspects of your life—but how *lucky* are you to own things that genuinely make you happy when you see them?

We often start projects asking if there's something in particular the client is passionate about in the space. In a pantry, sometimes people are avid bakers; in a closet, it might be their shoes they care about most; on bookshelves, it might be first edition novels they've been accumulating for years. Once we understand what someone cares about, we try to highlight it in a way that honors the collection. And we suggest you all do this in your own homes, because it's very gratifying. If you need help deciding whether something actually makes you happy, let's go through a little choose-your-own-adventure.

[THE] UNSCIENTIFIC GUIDE FOR MEASURING HUMAN HAPPINESS THROUGH INANIMATE OBJECTS

When you see the item . . .

1. You feel pleasantly satisfied. $\longrightarrow$ Hooray, it gets displayed.

2. You are glad you have it. $\longrightarrow$ Keep it stored safely.

3. You keep forgetting that you have it, but are *really* going to remember to use it this time. $\longrightarrow$ Okay . . . but the six-month clock has started ticking, and if it hasn't been used by then, it has to go.

4. You make a mental note to take it out when your stepmother comes over so she thinks you like it. $\longrightarrow$ Oh, come on, she doesn't care. Just give it to someone who *will* like it!

5. You are reminded about your to-do list item to get rid of things you don't need. $\longrightarrow$ WHAT ARE YOU WAITING FOR, AN INVITATION? Get rid of it! Sorry for yelling.

If you can confidently say your response to any particular item or items falls into category 1 or 2, then owning said item(s) purely because they make you happy is fine by us. In fact, it's encouraged.

IT'S OKAY TO OWN THINGS WHEN . . .

IN
HANDBAG
HEAVEN

We have a lot of empathy when it comes to owning more than a few handbags. In fact, we're not really the best people to help with a purse purge because we usually just say, "Sure, sure, sure, let's keep those." When it came to **Mandy Moore**'s closet, it only became more difficult to edit out items because everything was worthy of keeping. With no handbags on the chopping block, we decided to create a setup that highlighted her (and our!) favorites.

Step 1: Since it's pointless to cross the bridge halfway, we went all in and took over the center hanging rod and dresser top to devote to the various types of bags.

Step 2: Totes and handbags that could be hung were hooked onto the rod, while clutches and small purses were organized into acrylic dividers.

Step 3: We carefully chose a combination of open purse dividers and one enclosed version so that our favorite "MM" purse could sit perched on top.

THE
COOKBOOK
COLLECTOR

You know who really likes to cook? **Busy Philipps**. And her kids! It's really a whole family cooking affair in their kitchen, and as we moved through cabinets, drawers, and finally into the pantry, we realized they owned a lot of . . . everything. But sometimes, owning a lot of something gives us clues to what is meaningful in the space. It's kind of like an organizing Ouija board pointing us in the right direction. And we were being pointed straight toward loads and loads of cookbooks.

Step 1: Cookbooks that we had found on countertops, in cabinets, and on top of the fridge were piled up on the kitchen table while we unloaded the pantry components.

Step 2: While we wanted to highlight the cookbooks, we didn't want to compromise accessibility to the food in the pantry, so we arranged them on a high shelf in rainbow order.

Step 3: We used a combination of bins, turntables, and canisters to store all the food, but we were *also* able to use our custom Steele Canvas bins for overflow items.

true story

Sometimes (oftentimes?) kids are the biggest critics, so we held our breath when Busy's daughters, Birdie and Cricket, saw the pantry for the first time. THANK GOODNESS they liked it, because we were not leaving without their seal of approval.

LIFE IS BETTER WITH BEAUTY PRODUCTS

Some people are like us and have no business being in public without some foundation and lip gloss, but others genuinely love it. They enjoy owning every shade of lip gloss and endless eyeshadow palettes. We get it (even if we don't know how to actually use it all), and we're here to help. We used stacking modular drawers in this cabinet to help hold not just the sheer quantity of items, but also the variety of categories. No one is mixing up a lip liner and an eyeliner on our watch! All we ask is that someone kindly explain why "lip liner" is two words and "eyeliner" is one word—thanks!

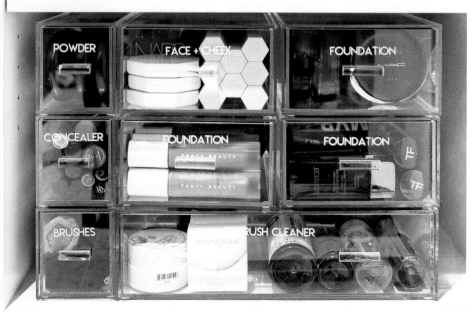

THE
SHOE
WALL

We like organizing most things, but there is nothing—NOTHING—more fun than a killer shoe collection. Red bottoms, studs, straps, 6-inch heels, every color in the rainbow: Bring it on, because we are here for it. And **Jessie James Decker** indeed brought it. In fact, she *kept* bringing it all the way from storage, and all of a sudden we were surrounded by huge boxes and an ocean of shoes and we were like, OKAY, FORGET WHAT WE SAID BEFORE, THIS IS ENOUGH, THANK YOU!

Step 1: We stand by our 80/20 rule *even* when it comes to shoes. And while we know Jessie loves her shoes, we had to convince her to part with just a few. Breathing room is always important when it comes to organization, but it's most critical when it's for a collection meant to be celebrated.

Step 2: Jessie is tiny, so we wanted to position her frequently used shoes closer to the bottom of the closet. With that in mind, we opted for a rainbow effect down the middle, and side stalls for black and neutral colors.

Step 3: Not all shoes are created equal. We stored the sneakers, slides, and slippers in baskets to keep them easily accessible but concealed from view.

This entire closet will forever live in THE hall of fame—but let's take a moment to reflect on the shoes. It was clear that not only was our client partial to certain brands, but when she found a style she liked, she also bought them in every color. So instead of arranging

them according to the rainbow, we grouped them by brand first, then by style, and finally by color. Sometimes color coordinating makes the most sense, and sometimes it doesn't! Take your cues from the shoes.

COLOR THERAPY

Color (and sometimes the absence of color) is a personal preference that dramatically varies from person to person. Some people feel connected to a palette of colors, and others gravitate toward one specific color. For whatever reason, that one shade makes them happier than others, and when we see the trend in someone's home, we lean in and showcase it. While organizing this singer and songwriter's closet, it was pretty obvious that color was yellow. We thought it would be fun to create some additional storage options to keep her favorite pieces visible.

Step 1: She tours quite a bit, so we had to dig through different bags, suitcases, closets, and drawers to corral her items.

Step 2: We knew we wanted to highlight her collection of yellow jewelry, but still wanted to keep *all* like items together. To accomplish this, the bracelet box was filled with yellow bangles, and the jewelry stacker was loaded with yellow sunglasses and jewelry on the top layers.

IT'S OKAY TO OWN THINGS WHEN . . .

Step 3: To accommodate larger accessories like clutches and belts, we installed an over-the-door unit with labeled hanging baskets. And of course we made sure to have all the yellow pieces poking out of the top!

Bobby Bones really loves red. He owns red clothes, red shoes, even red guitars. And since that's the color shoe he wears most often—particularly when performing—we kept those pairs on open shelves and stored the additional ones in shoeboxes on the top shelf.

In **Elsie Larson**'s home, she appreciates and *emphasizes* every color of the rainbow. When we came in to organize her kitchen, the wall of carefully curated glasses made us stop in our tracks. We had already seen it on Instagram, but seeing it in real life was something else entirely. So there was NO PRESSURE organizing the cabinets and drawers surrounding that masterpiece. At least we were able to style the shelves with complementary copper pieces to tie the two sides together.

true story

The first time we went to Elsie's house, we were so intimidated because every single room is more incredible than the next. When we got into the car afterward, we looked at each other and said, "If we're going to work in that house, we better figure out how to fake some actual talent ASAP."

BOOKWORM

Never have we ever told someone to get rid of a book. The only reason to purge a book is if you want to pass it on to someone else. Whether it's a novel you loved and want to share, or a baby book that your own children have outgrown, paying it forward is a great option. But here's our general rule of thumb: If you love books (and we hope you do), then keep every single one of them. They don't require batteries, are always there when you need them, and are the best decorating tool any house could have. While organizing **Lena Waithe**'s bookshelves, we took a bit of creative license and mixed up the traditional ROYGBIV pattern.

Step 1: You know the drill: ALL the books were piled ALL over the room. No room for walking, and yes, an absolute fire hazard.

Step 2: Surveying the stacks of books, it was clear that certain colors were more abundant than others. We decided on a configuration that would keep the colorful books in the middle, flanked by the black and white books on the ends. Books with spines that didn't cooperate with our well-thought-out plan were faced in the other direction to show the neutral pages instead.

Step 3: Storage boxes were placed on the lower shelves to blend in with the surrounding books.

IT MAKES YOU HAPPY

We love to organize books throughout the home, but they are always at their best in a kid's room. They add a bright pop of color and inspire your children to pick one up and read (or be read to). And while kids might not yet be able to alphabetize their books, they sure do know what the color green looks like! They will be able to find the book they're looking for, and put it back when they are done.

IT'S OKAY TO OWN THINGS WHEN . . .

HOBBIES
THAT MAKE
YOU HAPPY

Whether you enjoy gardening, playing the guitar, or knitting a blanket, it's nice to have a hobby. It's a brief pause from life's daily stresses, and we applaud anyone who learns a craft and practices it regularly.

Step 1: One of our favorite tricks for balls of yarn is to use clear magazine holders to store all the colors. We don't know how to knit, but can we count "creating yarn balls" as one of *our* hobbies?

Step 2: Sewing supplies were organized into a divided tea organizer (this is a good time to remind everyone to shop in ALL sections of the store, since you never know where you will find a good potential storage solution!).

Step 3: Instruments and knitting patterns are less fun to look at, so we organized them into concealed stackable bins.

For this *serious* yarn collection, we took over an entire shelving unit to hold every shade under the sun. We used file holders instead of magazine holders, since we needed larger containers.

THE
SENTIMENTAL
SPECTRUM

Sentimentality is experienced differently by everyone. It can range from wanting to keep EVERYTHING to just cherishing certain meaningful items. It can *even* take the form of owning only *one* sentimental item . . . a stuffed monkey named Gorilla (no good explanation for this) who sits on a closet shelf because *Toy Story* was very emotional and what if Gorilla couldn't breathe in a storage box? Just for instance. We all have our need to hold on to things we love or things given to us by people we love. As long as you are treating those items with respect, and not letting sentimental storage get out of hand, it's perfectly fine to save anything you deem special.

Hoda Kotb's closet is a good example of a middle-of-the-road sentimentalist. When we were purging her clothes, shoes, and handbags, there was an actual mountain of giveaway items on her bed. She was excellent at recognizing when she didn't need something, and we were SO PROUD. But there were a few things that struck a chord with her, and we wanted to put them front and center. We lined the top shelf with all her journals, and the bottom shelves with all her New Orleans Saints shirts, jerseys, and hats. We even let her keep multiples because (1) we are benevolent, and (2) we really, really, really love Hoda.

true story

While purging Hoda's closet, we extracted a mug stuffed with toddler socks, a handbag filled with crushed Pepcid AC and a toothbrush, and more than a few razors, so don't say this job isn't dangerous!

For **Khloé Kardashian**, our goal was to set up memory boxes to hold notes, cards, and keepsakes from her family and friends. Since we knew this collection was particularly meaningful to her, we wanted to make sure it was prominently displayed.

Step 1: Keepsakes come in all shapes and sizes, so we had to contend with what we could realistically display and what was necessary to store. Once we took stock of everything, we settled on displaying notes and cards, and storing bulkier items like memorabilia.

Step 2: When all the categories were separated (parents, siblings, friends, etc.), we used clear acrylic containers to keep everything visible and added a light pink label to each for an extra-special touch.

Step 3: Khloé's *own* stationery was placed in the middle so she could easily send someone a note.

The most common solution we use for sentimental storage is a set of document boxes. They can hold anything from cards to concert tickets, kids' artwork to a high school diploma. For items bigger than a bread box, we go with a tall square version that can accommodate bulkier pieces.

For larger sentimental items, a bookcase can hold everything in one place, and double for décor. Subtle displays of significant items help to keep things we love in our daily thoughts. And if you love them, you probably want to look at them as often as possible.

true story

The framed "one" sat on Clea and John's table at their wedding, the cameras belonged to her grandfather, and of course . . . there's a framed photo of her grandma Ruthie's iconic glasses.

IT'S OKAY TO OWN THINGS WHEN . . .

The *FINISHING* TOUCHES

Remember when we said you always need to start with smart systems and *then* work to make it pretty? Well, now that we've covered all those smart systems, it's time for dessert. Form meeting function is our specialty, and we want to share some of our favorite tips and tricks.

Always create a focal spot. Or what we also refer to as a "moment." Even the smallest touch can make a space shine. Consider everything from a canister collection in a pantry to a handbag displayed in a closet:

- Clear canisters of snacks or other dry goods centered on a pantry shelf
- A favorite handbag displayed in a closet on an acrylic riser
- Art supplies or books sorted in ROYGBIV on a playroom shelf
- A statement piece with personality (i.e., cactus heels or a painting of Elvis Presley, both of which are proudly displayed in **Kacey Musgraves**'s closet!)

Be spatially aware. Look at the *entire* space before implementing anything. You want to make sure you are taking advantage of all available room evenly.

- Think in odd numbers: 3 baskets on a shelf look a lot better than 4. If you need to fill the space, center the baskets and spread them out evenly.
- If you can stack, stack—but always think about visual weight and distribution beforehand. You don't want things to look lopsided or top heavy.

- Allow some breathing room. Negative space can be a good thing, especially when it gives you room to grow (remember the 80/20 rule?).
- Use clear containers to add depth and make a small space appear larger.

Uniformity is key. Pick your products wisely and *consistently.* Having mismatched pieces makes a space look disheveled and disconnected.
- Determine the aesthetic of your home or space and let that style lead your shopping decisions.
- Pay attention to the smaller details like type of handle and textures. If you decide to mix products, just make sure the items look intentional together and don't confuse the eye.
- Mirror same or similar items to create balance in a room (aka symmetry!). To avoid monotony, play around with varying heights and shapes—as long as the two items look somewhat similar, they'll balance each other out.

ROYGBIV whenever possible. If it makes sense, go ahead and line things up according to the rainbow. Many times, this is part of a functional system, but sometimes . . . it's just for fun.

Add a label. Much like the rainbow, most of the time a label is part of a system that helps keep the space organized. But sometimes, a label can be used just for its aesthetic value and that's okay, too. The better a space looks, the more likely you are to maintain it.

Wipe down surfaces. It may seem obvious, but cleaning your room—especially the windows and glass cabinets—goes a long way in making a space feel tidier.

Thanks

Joanna, thank you for being my other half. I wouldn't have been able to get through a single day without you. John, sorry you are second in the acknowledgments, but you're first in my heart. Now I feel like I owe Joanna an apology because I can already hear her say, "What, am I not in your heart too?" I can't win. I love you both.

To Stella and Sutton, you are my pride and joy, the loves of my life, and I'm so grateful to be your mom. And before you tell me that I listed you third and forth on here—I went in alphabetical order. To my family and friends, I'm sorry I haven't been great on text lately, I promise I'll do better next year!

—Clea

First, I want to thank you, Clea! Not only are you an unstoppable business partner and one of my most favorite people of all time but you, alone, have the dedication, drive, design eye, and incredible talent of compiling our combined mindsets and The Home Edit methods into a beautiful, funny, informative, inspiring, well-organized narrative.

I would also like to thank my other partner in life, Jeremy. Thank you for marrying me thirteen years ago, being the top parent for schools to call in case of emergencies, and for being my rock.

Lastly, Miles and Marlowe, thank you for embracing your third sibling, The Home Edit, as I know how needy she can sometimes be, for all of us. Your acceptance and understanding of her never goes unnoticed.

—Joanna

INDEX

An Hachette UK Company
www.hachette.co.uk

First published in Great Britain in 2020 by Mitchell Beazley,
an imprint of Octopus Publishing Group Ltd
Carmelite House
50 Victoria Embankment
London EC4Y 0DZ
www.octopusbooks.co.uk

ISBN 978-1-78472-716-1

A CIP catalogue record for this book is available from
the British Library.

Printed in Italy

Book design by Mia Johnson
Photography by Clea Shearer

10 9 8 7 6 5